COMPETITION, FAIRNESS, AND EQUALITY IN SPORT AND SOCIETY

COMPETITION, FAIRNESS, AND EQUALITY IN SPORT AND SOCIETY

VERNER MØLLER

First published in 2022
as part of the *Sport and Society Book Imprint*
doi: 10.18848/978-1-957792-02-6/CGP (Full Book)

Common Ground Research Networks
University of Illinois Research Park
2001 South First St, Suite 201 L
Champaign, IL 61820 USA

Copyright © Verner Møller 2022

All rights reserved. Apart from fair dealing for the purposes of study, research, criticism or review as permitted under the applicable copyright legislation, no part of this book may be reproduced by any process without written permission from the publisher.

Library of Congress Cataloging-in-Publication Data

Names: Møller, Verner, author.
Title: Competition, fairness, and equality in sport and society / Verner
   Møller.
Description: Champaign, IL : Common Ground Research Networks, 2022. |
   Series: Sharp Ideas ; volume 1 | Includes bibliographical references. |
   Summary: "Competition is a basic fact of life. Life in the modern world,
   based on rationality, ingenuity, and co-operative skills, makes it easy
   to forget this and to believe that it no longer applies to human beings.
   Developments in the western world since the turn of the millennium
   appear to confirm this perception. Competition, fairness, and equality
   in sport and society aims to show that this interpretation is wrong.
   Based on the workings of elite sport, it argues that the fairness and
   equality agenda, rather than being a manifestation of a mellowing of
   human nature, is essentially driven by the same innate competitive
   impulses. What has changed is that, once basic material needs for
   survival are covered, as is the case in the developed world, people
   continue to compete in other arenas attempting to improve their position
   in the human hierarchies and win status and recognition"-- Provided by
   publisher.
Identifiers: LCCN 2022011247 (print) | LCCN 2022011248 (ebook) | ISBN
   9781957792002 (Hardback : alk. paper) | ISBN 9781957792019 (Paperback :
   alk. paper) | ISBN 9781957792026 (pdf)
Subjects: LCSH: Sports--Sociological aspects. | Sports--Moral and ethical
   aspects. | Sex discrimination in sports. | Racism in sports. |
   Competition (Psychology)
Classification: LCC GV706.5 .M63 2022 (print) | LCC GV706.5 (ebook) | DDC
   306.4/83--dc23
LC record available at https://lccn.loc.gov/2022011247
LC ebook record available at https://lccn.loc.gov/2022011248

SHARP IDEAS

The book series "Sharp Ideas in Sport" is aimed to advance existing contemporary discussions on sport and body culture through providing critical debates and challenging perspectives. The series is established with the ambition to create a hub for controversial, radical, and provocative views that challenge current insights into global sport. The concise pocket book format allows the general public to access our books but equally informs academic debate.

The rationale for the series stems from a trend in academia and wider society that controversial thoughts and arguments are often neglected in favor of popular or uncontentious views. Books, academic articles, and contributions to anthologies on sensitive topics that have merit but are socially or ideologically offensive are often suppressed. Such moral culture in scholarly work threatens the academic freedom that is supposed to perpetuate the status quo in our societies and therewith the future of our university institutions.

"Sharp Ideas in Sport" provides a forum that is detached from mainstream political and ideological viewpoints, and open for anyone who wants to confront mainstream as well as unconventional ideas based on reason and coherent arguments. A double-blinded peer-review process ensures the consistency of arguments, but authors are invited to argue against criticism if they believe the reviewers' verdicts are influenced by political or ideological views.

The book series thus aims to help readers to understand divisive issues in sport better through indiscriminate presentation of arguments of clearly defined sides, including those that do not match with the predominant narrative of being "correct". Our hope is that this will stimulate readers to sharpen their own critical thinking.

Verner Møller and Jörg Krieger

TABLE OF CONTENTS

Editor's Commentary	*XIII*
Foreword	*XVII*
Introduction	1
The Concept of Fairness	11
Rights	37
Equal Pay	51
Athletes, Gender, and the Free Market	65
Women and Sport	79
Conclusion	101
References	*105*

EDITOR'S COMMENTARY

Competition, Fairness, and Equality in Sport and Society by Verner Møller will unquestionably divide opinions. In the current climate of emotionally charged debates on sex and gender in sport, the book presents arguments that are in direct opposition to many of the mainstream viewpoints we are reading about these days. In some cases, those arguments are entirely opposed or censored before they are even presented. This happened, for example, at the *Humboldt-Universität zu Berlin* in summer 2022, where a talk on gender and biology had been cancelled due to protests of student groups. The cancellation led to concerns by ministers and academics alike, highlighting that universities are places of intellectual contests and should not be forced by activists to decide which positions are presented and which not. The incident highlighted that we live in a time in which ideas are immediately radicalized and exchanges of arguments are – if they even take place – fueled by ideological or political standpoints. We can agree with the viewpoints of the protesters, but their opposition to contrasting arguments should not result in censoring.

This book, however, is published in the "Sharp Ideas" book series that aims to present controversial viewpoints and aims to counteract such developments. The book series' is Verner Møller's initiative and *Competition, Fairness, and Equality in Sport and Society* has the objective to present to readers and potential future authors the format of the series. The book series aims to widen the space for academic discourse within the area of sport studies as we believe that discussions are not enriched by chasing after a narrow canon of opinions, but by contradiction and the willingness to weigh up arguments. Such an attitude will strengthen a democratic and academic culture of debate.

Being sharp and provocative does not mean that we can just throw at each other unsubstantiated arguments. Academic debates need conflict, and they also need a minimum of balance and respect. If we argue only normatively, without the necessary expertise, and without taking into consideration the latest research and key literature, our academic debate culture will be violated and potentially misused. This is the reason for my selection of reviewers for this manuscript, for which I had full and sole responsibility. I made a conscious decision for the book to be reviewed by international experts in the field of gender in sport who have widely published feminist viewpoints. The book was also thoroughly reviewed by the publisher's editorial team. Our rational was to challenge Verner Møller's ideas and provoke him to reconsider and strengthen his arguments. He has fulfilled this task and even though he does not agree with the reviewers, he engaged in-depth with their arguments. We asked the reviewers whether their reviews can be published anonymously together with the author's response in an online review section of this book series. One reviewer has agreed, and I highly recommend anyone who reads this book to carefully go through the review and the response. It will contribute to a better understanding of the presented arguments and viewpoints.

Finally, I would like to highlight that the views presented in the book are not my personal opinions, nor those of the Sport and Society Research Network (of which I am the chair), nor the views of our publisher. However, I consider it my duty as an editor of this book series to present different perspectives so arguments can be weighed against each other. I appreciate that our publisher, Common Ground Research Networks, has supported my intentions with this series. It is not my role to act as a censor because I might have different views, but to assess whether an author argues substantially and logically. In fact, the books published within the Sport and Society Research Network Book Imprint, and especially the recently launched the Teaching Book Series, provide a variety of perspectives in an attempt to find the right balance for an informed academic debate. Amongst the first teaching books are *Sport and Hegemony* and *Women in the Olympics*, both standing in stark contrast to some of the arguments presented in the book on hand. The Sport & Society Research Network is a place in which scholars should be able to present their theses, research results, and viewpoints freely to discussion. This book and this book series will hopefully further contribute to that.

Jörg Krieger,
Sport & Society Research Network Chair

FOREWORD

The book you are about to read is out of step with the *zeitgeist*. This was reflected in the peer reviews it received. According to one of the reviewers, the book presents views that "are clearly in the minority" and "so outdated and unpopular, as they are based on conservative Christian and gender critical beliefs, not cogent arguments". Despite the reviewers' general dissatisfaction with the book's content, they nonetheless contributed some useful observations and suggestions that I am grateful for. I have incorporated those into the text.

I believe that a researcher's political views should be irrelevant to his or her analytical work. Previously it would never have occurred to me to reveal my political convictions in an academic text. The insights gained from studying a topic may shape researchers political views and influence how they vote, but to let their research be colored by political preferences would be entirely unprofessional. Yet, since one of the reviewers apparently reads the book as a conservative Christian and gender-critical text, it seems appropriate to reveal that I have always voted center-left, considered myself an atheist, and am all for gender equality. So, the accusation that my ideas are based on conservative Christian and gender critical beliefs was surprising, to say the least.

The problem of bias is well-known. People are inclined to accept arguments, views and findings that confirm their own position more easily than oppositional ones. But, since I do not hold the Christian conservative views the reviewer believes s/he has uncovered, and since in all likelihood our political views are not poles apart, it is worth considering what provoked this reviewer to the extent that s/he admits: "I kept stopping to reflect on whether or not I was letting my own perspectives and very strong negative reaction to several sections cloud my analysis." The reviewer's proposal to rename the book "something like, 'A Conservative Christian and Gender Critical Perspective on Competition…" leads me to think that its actual title aroused in the reviewer expectations of a reassuring tome that would affirm her personal views on fairness and equality in sport and society, that such expectations may have been frustrated, and that this frustration may have found expression in her assessment. For instead of a more predictable analysis of the injustices standing in the way of fairness and equality in sport and society, the book argues that a fair and equal world is unlikely ever to come about, given the competitive nature of life. The implication being that efforts currently made to this end in the form of, say, identity politics can only be in vain. The reviewer's immediate disappointment with the content, left her seemingly unable or unwilling to read the manuscript on its own premises. Had s/he read the book on its own terms, s/he would have realized from the way the kingdom of heaven is painted in it that the manuscript could not have been authored by a Christian believer. Both reviewers find the speculation about a paradisical afterlife strange in a book about sport and society, so it seems apt to prepare the reader by explaining that the kingdom of heaven represents the ideal place where the condition of human equality is finally achieved. Such a place, I argue, is not human at all.

Since I am not a Christian conservative, there must be another reason why the reviewer deems the present analysis "outdated" and "unpopular". My sense is that it comes down to differences in epistemology, so it might be relevant to briefly describe my analytical background. I was enrolled as a university student in the early 1980s. Critical theory of the so-called Frankfurt School was a favored analytical framework within the humanities and social sciences. At the heart of this theory was a critique of capitalist society. Using a methodological critique of ideology, we learned to expose the ideological underpinnings of capitalist society designed to hide the disparity of interests pursued by the elite and the lower classes. The underlying premise was that societal wealth was distributed unfairly. As hard-up students, we could identify with this as an analysis. One book that made lasting impact was *Dialektik der Aufklärung* (Dialectic of Enlightenment) a collection of essays by the director of the Frankfurt School of Social Research, Max Horkheimer, and Theodor W. Adorno. Writing against the backdrop of the rise of Nazism, these authors were profoundly skeptical about the potency of reason. In their view, the attack on the authority of the Church that took place in the Age of Reason had had serious negative consequences. Their main criticisms related to human alienation. Enlightenment thinking paved the way for modern positivist science that enabled humans to master nature but, as a result, led to a disenchantment of the world and left modern man with no meaning but as a consumer. Moreover, the technological innovations that this science inspired worked as a fertilizer for capitalism, as they led to rational means of mass production that made consumer society possible and developed means of mass communication that proved effective in seducing people to believe in consumption as the meaning of life. Horkheimer and Adorno did not forsake reason per se but did not trust it as a bulwark against irrational impulses. The culture industry – not to be confused with the fine arts – undermined the authority of the educated and of well-founded expertise (Horkheimer & Adorno, 1969). The expansion of this industry together with the advent of social media have demonstrated the long-lasting relevance of critical theory. The observation that a critical analysis of the unholy alliance between popular culture and capitalism is not sufficient for humans and that they also need something to believe in is as valuable as ever.

Another favored theoretical framework at the time was postmodern cultural and social constructivism. Like the Frankfurt School, postmodernist thinkers were critical of modernity, but they took their criticism much further. They were not only skeptical of science and the modern narrative of progress. The socialist alternatives around the world had in many cases been unmasked as brutal regimes with little appeal. The lack of successful alternatives to capitalism resulted in a nihilist attitude among proponents of postmodern thought. Instead of criticizing, like the Frankfurt School the side-effects of modernity in the hope that profound critique would lead to its correction, they spent their time and effort breaking down, or "deconstructing", as it was called, the mainstays of modern science. Language was rendered unreliable, although at the same time presented as immensely powerful. Reality did not shape language. It was the other way round. Language shaped reality. The way we speak about things shapes what we know and how we think. That is, the human mind is shackled by discourses produced and controlled by a hegemonic system consisting of schools, the media, law, science, bureaucracy and so on. In accordance with this, concepts such as reality, truth, logic, objective facts, universals, absolutes, essence were rejected and replaced by a new set of mysteriously esoteric concepts like hyperreality, simulacrum, potentiality, performativity, language games, *différence*, hypertext, and many more.

It was an obscure world to come to grips with. But it was taught, and I believed in it, learned to master the jargon and it paid off. I got appointed at the university and taught postmodern theory to my students. Household names on the reading list were Jean Baudrillard, Francois Lyotard, Jacques Derrida, Gilles Deleuze Felix Guattari, and Kenneth Gergen among others. True to their critique of reason, logic, and language these authors excelled in writing ambiguous abstract sentences spiced up with neologisms and technical terms and concepts from the natural sciences. The students could not make head or tail of most of these texts, but they were fascinated by the dissolution of the reality they knew. Take this mind-blowing example from the introduction to Baudrillard's *Seduction*:

> Seduction continues to appear to all orthodoxies as malefice and artifice, a black magic for the deviation of all truths, an exaltation of the malicious use of signs, a conspiracy of signs. Every discourse is threatened with this sudden reversibility, absorbed into its own signs without a trace of meaning. This is why all disciplines, which have as an axiom the coherence and finality of their discourse, must try to exorcize it. This is where seduction and femininity are confounded, indeed, confused. Masculinity has always been haunted by this sudden reversibility within the feminine. Seduction and femininity are ineluctable as the reverse side of sex, meaning and power. (Baudrillard, 1990, p. 2)

It was a sort of sorcery, the world re-enchanted. As a young teacher it was to a certain degree gratifying to elucidate some of the deeper insights hidden under the surface. But the gratification lasted only so long. Occasionally brave students admitted that they neither understood the text nor my interpretation and asked me to make it simpler. This was terribly uncomfortable, because I could only reiterate in oracular fashion what they had already heard. It was impossible to provide clear, logical, common-sense explanations, because the texts were produced without following rules of logic and common sense. Doubt set in. It dawned upon me that the opaque parts of the postmodernists' writings might be nothing more than a nonsensical academic form of play-acting of little relevance to the world in which the students would work after graduation. At academic conferences, I began to test this hypothesis, asking postmodern presenters naïve questions like the ones I had been asked by my students. I noticed that questions such as, "You say there is no truth, is that true?" annoyed presenters, and aroused displeasure in the audience. A postmodern historian claimed that history was merely a set of novel-like narratives. To the question whether the two genres were not different in the sense that good history attempts to give a true account of the past whereas good novels can be pure fantasy, the historian answered: "I don't believe in truth with a capital T." This pseudo-answer was applauded like a goal scored. A similar gaffe was provided by a postmodern gender researcher who claimed that sex differences (not gender roles) were socially constructed. In answer to the question why half of humankind had constructed a world that made them subordinate to the other half in the first place, she replied: "Women's subordination has evolved in a historical process determined by a patriarchal system of power." This may sound reasonable on the surface, but such patriarchal power cannot be detached from human agency and, by extension, from differences of sex.

Increasingly discontent with such lack of clarity and consistency, my fascination of postmodern theory waned. I shelved postmodern literature and began seeking inspiration in sociological classics such as Emilé Durkheim, Marcel Mauss, Max Weber, Karl Mannheim and C. Wright Mills, whose revelations of original thinking were presented in masterly clear prose. *The Sociological Imagination* by Mills was truly liberating. Some of his advice seems more pertinent than ever in academia today, where people excel in what Mills urges us to avoid:

> Avoid any rigid set of procedures. Above all, seek to develop the sociological imagination. Avoid the fetishism of method and technique. Urge the rehabilitation of the unpretentious intellectual craftsman [...] Be one mind that is on its own confronting the problems of man and society. Avoid the Byzantine oddity of associated and disassociated Concepts, the mannerism of verbiage. Urge upon yourself and upon others the simplicity of clear statement. Use more elaborated terms only when you believe firmly that their use enlarges the scope of your sensibilities, the precision of your references, the depth of your reasoning. [...] Examine in detail little facts and their relations, and big unique events as well. But do not be fanatic: relate all such work, continuously and closely, to the level of historical reality. [...] Take as your task, the defining of this reality, formulate your problems in its terms; on its level try to solve these problems and thus resolve the issues and the troubles they incorporate. And never write more than three pages without at least having in mind a solid example. (Mills, 2000 (1959), p. 224)

Following this advice, I have given up postmodern constructivism and assumed realism as the starting point for my analyzes. This, of course, does not mean that I have lost sight of the fact that many things in life are social and cultural constructions. Money, marriage, law, tournaments, religion, and art are just a few examples. But this is a rather banal insight. It is easy to understand that a piece of paper with a picture of Benjamin Franklin and $100 written on it will not keep you warm for long on a lonely island, although it could be exchanged to a considerable stack of firewood at Walmart. But it does not make sense to maintain that the tree that delivered the material to both the note and the firewood was also constructed or that your bodily need to keep warm is. So, I take for granted that beneath our constructions there is a brute reality that is not constructed.

In line with this, I accept that language is a construction. It is constructed as a tool that allows us to communicate about our experiences in and of the world. Language makes thinking possible. It is arbitrary that we call one thing a stick and another thing a snake. It could have been the other way around. But our species has been well served by our ability to agree on what each term referred to as it could be fatal to mix them up. Reality does not change because we change the concepts we use about various phenomena. A stick does not become poisonous if we call it a snake, and a snake, if we pick it up, will react in accordance with its nature no matter if we called it a stick. By the same token, a man will never give birth to a child even if he insists he is a woman, and a woman will never make another woman pregnant using her own semen. Attempts to change the brute reality by changing the meaning of concepts or the way we use language get nowhere. They only cause confusion and makes reasoning harder. So, I use language in a straightforward everyday manner. Therefore, when you read the heading: "Protection of the weaker sex", you do not need to wonder, as one of the reviewers did, whether I mean the marginalized sex or refer to the second sex in Simone de Beauvoir's sense. It simply means the physically weaker sex. And yes, I am aware that many women in the world are physically stronger than many men. And yes, I know that women on average live longer than men so that their physiology in that sense is more robust. I do trust, however, that readers who read the essay with an open mind will be able to understand the words I use without having the meaning spelled out.

Having said that, I should perhaps clarify how I understand elite sport since this is a core concept in the text and both reviewers seem to have problems with my interpretation. When I think of elite sport, I think of a construction characterized by the following four criteria:

1. The activity is played out as a competition, which is taken seriously even though it serves no external purpose, and in that sense can be regarded as not serious.
2. The aim is to win and to move upwards within the activity's hierarchical structure.
3. The activity is organized and functions in an institutionalized framework, in which results are recorded and are ascribed significance.
4. The activity is governed by a written set of rules, which are administered by a judge who ideally is impartial.

The *raison d'etre* of elite sport, as I understand it, is about winning and moving up in the sports hierarchy. On this basis I maintain that, "it is consistent with the very nature of competitive sport that rivals should want to overpower their opponents and see them suffer defeat." In addition, I maintain that sport exposes the brutal truth that equality among humans is an illusion.

The reviewers, apparently resistant to relinquishing their hopes for an equal society, challenges this understanding of sport by asking: "if competition only serve to show inequality, what happens when football ends in a draw or when luck or bad weather plays a deciding role." Apart from the fact that I do not say that competition only shows inequality, these are good questions. In fact, all football matches begin as a draw and often end in a draw. This means that the two teams get a point each and their rivals, winning in other matches, can benefit from this result and move up the table. If two teams end the Premier League with the same number of points, the winner is decided on goal difference. If the goal difference is the same, the team that has scored most goals wins. It is only if the teams still cannot be separated that they will be declared joint champions, which is not a situation that has so far happened in the history of the league. As regards luck and bad weather, these phenomena clearly play a role in life. Some people are lucky in sports and in life in general. Some starve and freeze to death due to bad weather conditions. This happens to people all the time, including people who have all the physical and mental resources to succeed in life if they had grown up somewhere else. This only goes to show that inequality is a fact of life, and that competition does not always take place on equal and fair terms.

INTRODUCTION

It is often said that sport is a reflection of society, that it mirrors life. There are good reasons for this. Elite sport is about competition. Athletic performances are measured, athletes are ranked and those who excel are in many cases handsomely rewarded. The same is true for modern life in general. All else being equal, those who get the best grades in high school have easier access to the most prestigious courses of further or higher education and afterwards – if they perform well – to the most lucrative jobs. Landing a job does not mean that competition is over. In recent decades the luxury of tenure has come under pressure. Short-term contracts, which is the norm in sports, have become more and more common; and in all walks of life even employees on permanent contracts are increasingly being measured, compared, and pushed to the limit of their capacities (Standing, 2014). Some people are robust enough to continue unaffected by this new life condition. Some even find grades, scoreboards, and bonus schemes motivating. Yet, the intensified emphasis on individual competitiveness has resulted in an increase in mental issues. Younger people who have not established a firm foothold in life seem particularly prone (Gander, 2019). The negative consequences of intensified competition are also to be found in relation to sport. It would be difficult to imagine anyone reach an elite level without discovering some enjoyment in competing.

But not all elite athletes thrive in their competitive sports environments. Many have been identified as extraordinarily talented at a tender age. Some of these have been lured by immediate success and the recognition that comes with it. But as they climb the ladder, competition gets fiercer, and their superiority diminishes, they find it increasingly hard to cope. In some cases the competitive environment causes elite level athletes to suffer from stress, depression, anxiety, and panic attacks (Ingle, 2019). Similar consequences are found among students and employees in their respective competitive environments. Some of the coping mechanisms are also similar, whether they take the form of stimulants, performance enhancing medication or early retirement, while others try to get through by fraudulent means. The many *similarities* between sport and society at large make sport a valuable subject of study in order to learn about the effects and side-effects of intensified competition, which has become a fact of life in the age of globalization.

Elite sport is also useful as a tool to analyze developmental trajectories in contemporary western society due to its deviations from overall societal developments. The simple and somewhat cynical reality of elite sport offers sobering perspectives on many hotly debated topics in modern society. Thus, it can serve as a magnifying glass, allowing us to see aspects often neglected, hidden or denied for ideological reasons. My ambition with this essay is to demonstrate the value of applying an elite sport perspective when analyzing current societal issues. The underlying hypothesis is that competition is the essence of capitalism and that it permeates human life in the global capitalist world. Even the most competition averse people are subject to it. As a result, human activity in all arenas play out in ways akin to elite sport. The problem of course is that the rules are not always so clear and chances of success are seldom fairly distributed. As regards the latter this is also true for elite sports.

There is a long tradition for viewing (elite) sport as a character-building enterprise. This is reflected in the notion sportsmanship for instance and in the Olympic creed formulated by the founder of the modern Olympics Pierre de Coubertin: "The important thing in the Olympic Games is not winning but taking part, just as in life, what counts is not the victory but the struggle" (Coubertin, 2000, p. 587). It should be reminded, though, that these words were inspired by bishop Ethelbert Talbot. In a sermon in Saint Paul's Cathedral during the 1908 London Olympics attended by Olympic athletes and officials, Talbot reflected on the implications of the Games and notes that:

> ...young men of robust physical life have come from all parts of the world. It does mean, I think, as someone has said, that this era of internationalism as seen in the Stadium has an element of danger. Of course, it is very true, as he says, that each athlete strives not only for the sake of sport, but for the sake of his country. Thus a new rivalry is invented. If England be beaten on the river, or America outdistanced on the racing path, or that American has lost the strength which she once possessed. Well what of it? The only safety after all lies in the lesson of the real Olympia – that the Games themselves are better than the race and the price (sic!). St. Paul tells us how insignificant is the prize. Our prize is not corruptible, but incorruptible, and though only one may wear the laurel wreath, all may share the equal joy of the contest. All encouragement, therefore, be given to the exhilarating – I might say soul-saving – interested that comes in active and fair and clean athletic sports. (Widlund, 1994, p. 10)

The 1908 Games took place in a time of growing international rivalry. England's domination of world trade was waning while America was on the rise. The Grand Duchy of Finland wanted independence from Russia and refused to follow the Russian's demand that the Finns should carry the Russian flag during the march of nations. Ireland was not content either after being told that their victories were to be tallied with the British. Unsurprisingly, in this atmosphere, the international rivalries led to intensified on field competition, instances of foul play, controversy and protests. Unaffected by the core idea that it is individuals not nations that compete, the Olympics were used, as so often since, for nationalistic purposes as a competition between nation states (Matthews, 1980).

So, when Talbot addressed the danger of robust young men gathered to compete in a Stadium in the era of internationalism it was because he worried that hostilities might increase further. He wanted sporting contests to be fair and clean. Talbot's words could be heard as an attempt to evoke a Christian spirit of sport: an ideal of fairness and equality where young athletes enjoy competition in a friendly atmosphere of mutual respect and recognition. This "soul-saving" attitude should protect the attending athletes against the temptation of what in this context might be appropriately referred to as the devilish essence of elite sport. That is, the sporting reality where athletic ability to dominate and defeat opponents is hailed and victors are celebrated, emphasizing human inequality and fertilizing sentiments of superiority. Although Talbot's words made a lasting impression by the high hopes they expressed of a peaceful world where everybody was recognized and competition was for fun, the reality of the Games did not live up to this ideal, and was proven a pipe dream less than a decade later by the outbreak of World War I.

Because all humans do not share the same ideals, values, and beliefs convictions of this kind often give rise to harsh exchanges of opinions. Occasionally they move people to commit physical violence and ultimately ignite armed wars. In keeping with the competitive nature of humankind there is often a remarkable discrepancy between humans' ideals and their course of action as this essay will show. It is uplifting to listen to ideals like those expressed by Talbot. Sadly, they usually fall short in the real world. In truth, there are compelling evidence that humankind is becoming less violent and is improving in moral terms. There are fewer wars, homicides, rapes, beatings, less child abuse and bullying while at the same time we see an improvement in women's rights, children's rights, minority rights, and animal rights (Pinker, 2012). However, improvements in these respects have not come about miraculously. They also seem a result of our willingness to fight for a course. Much of the progress we today take for granted has been established by institutional force, military deterrence or fought for by human rights activists, and is still in many respects being opposed, tested and contested.

In recent years identity politics has been high on the agenda. Gender inequality, racism, homo- and transphobia has moved from the fringe toward the center of public attention. The rainbow flag has become a symbol of freedom and equal rights. The use of the symbolic rainbow colors as captain's armbands and shoelaces has been promoted by the English Premier League as a sign of the organization's commitment to diversity, tolerance, and inclusion. During the UEFA European 2020 Championship (played in 2021 due to the Covid-19 postponement), the German goalkeeper Manuel Neuer also demonstrated his commitment to the LGBT+ course when, against the protocol, he replaced the captain's armband officially provided by UEFA with a rainbow colored one. The tournament was even used by the car company Volkswagen to launch a pro-LGBT+ advertising campaign with rainbow-colored banners on the stadia's advertising boards. Following police officer Derek Chauvin's murder of George Floyd, another conspicuous anti-discrimination manifestation spread across the sporting world, as former National Football League quarterback Colin Kaepernick's "taking the knee" gesture against racism was widely adopted. This gesture, seen by some as yet another manifestation of identity politics, was widespread during the same European Championship. Scotland, Wales, Belgium, Portugal, and Switzerland among others took the knee before some or all of their games. Prior to the tournament, England's national coach, Gareth Southgate, announced that his players would take the knee before all their games. He stressed that the team's action was not a manifestation of support for the Black Lives Matter movement, which would have made it a political statement: "We have got a situation where some people think it is a political stand that they don't agree with. That is not the reason the players are doing it. We are supporting each other" (BBC News, 2021). Southgate's message was clear. As a multiracial team at a time when interracial tensions seem to be intensifying, the gesture was simply a sign of solidarity and team spirit among the English players. It was meant to include and unite, not to divide people. Nonetheless, the gesture was not appreciated by all fans. Some fans booed it, and Conservative MPs maintained that Southgate's comments were an "insult to the fans' intelligence" and that the FA was making a big mistake by alienating supporters through its support of a left-wing political movement (J. Murray, 2021). So, whether intended or not, taking the knee has become a political football. Many of those taking the knee or waving the rainbow flag would, no doubt, claim to be acting in the name of equality and fairness of opportunity.

Alongside the visible in-stadia manifestations of support for anti-racism and LGBT+ rights, gender inequality in sports in relation to salary, prize money, media coverage etc. is also the subject of intense debate. A growing number of male sports stars have used their platforms to voice support for the women's cause, and in 2017 Nike launched its equality campaign: "Until we all win", which emphasized that, "Nike believes in the power of sport to unite and inspire people to take action in their communities. Equality isn't a game. But achieving it will be our greatest victory. Until we all win" (Nike, 2017).

Whereas the original conflict in capitalist society has been between the economic elite, owners of land, property, and means of production on the one hand and the working class on the other, it appears that new battlelines are being drawn up. People – privileged and unprivileged alike – join together to fight for a vision of global tolerance, inclusion and equality across sex, ethnicity, religion, and occupation and against what they identify as reactionary bigotry. Notably, this alliance, based on identity politics, has formed at a moment in history when economic inequality between rich and poor countries and between rich and poor people within these countries has never been greater and is growing by the minute (Piketty, 2017).

It is hard to imagine that Volkswagen, which was caught in a massive emission fraud scandal in 2019 when it was revealed that the company had installed emission software designed to cheat the pollution test in more than ten million cars sold worldwide, are powered by the same motives as the LGBT+ community. That Nike, who in 2020 paid their CEO a total of $53 million and nine more executives on average $12 million while at the same time outsourcing their production to sweatshops in developing countries where, according to a 2018 report, they pay "poverty" wages to workers, are overly committed to equality (New Idea, 2019). Or that all footballers in the Premier League who continue collectively to take the knee before matches are suddenly on the same page politically and are equally passionate about this form of protest. For sure, many footballers are outspoken against racism and are strongly committed to the cause, and there may be few, if any, who share the ideology of Italian Paolo Di Canio, a declared fascist who played in the Premier League 1997-2004. But there is reason to believe that some of the kneeling players are doing it half-heartedly and would prefer not to. In fact, Crystal Palace's Wilfried Zaha, the first player in the Premier League to proclaim he would stop taking the knee, justified his decision by saying that he found it degrading. And Brentford's Ivan Toney explained why the entire Brentford team had decided to stop making the anti-racism gesture, saying that the players felt they were being used as puppets so "people at the top" could "rest on the subject and nothing has changed as a result" (Thomas, 2021).

As a company, it is valuable to have an image customers can identify with. Hence it makes good sense to position oneself in line with the trends of the time. This does not, of course, mean that the observable alignment between apparently progressive companies and social and political movements heralds an era in which competition will cease in favor of a harmonious world of equality, tolerance, and inclusion. Rather than being a sign of genuine commitment to social justice, the current embracing by companies and football clubs of social justice movements may well be a result of calculated marketing strategies, by which they try to gain an edge in a competitive market.

As will be clear from what follows, competition is a basic condition in life. It pervades human existence whether we like it or not. People even have competing views on the meaning of fairness and equality and how it should be ensured, as discussions within sport and society in the 21st century reveal. I open this essay with an examination of an exchange of views by female cyclists about transwomen's eligibility to take part in women's sports in the wake of a transwoman's victory in the Masters Track Cycling World Championships in 2018. It should be noted that I use this example solely because it is well-suited to illuminate the concept of fairness. That is, I do not in this essay examine the issue of transgender athletes' participation in sport.

Fairness is related to, but by no means synonymous with, equality. Some argue that it is fair to treat people equally even if it leads to unequal outcomes; other argue that it is fair to treat people unequally in order to enable equal outcomes. After examining the concept of fairness, I turn my attention to equality. This ideal, formulated in declarations of human rights, has been important in the development of Western democracy. It is therefore no wonder that this ideal has also been promoted in the context of sport, even though sport quite obviously demonstrates the opposite: that people are unequal. In recent years the ideal of equality has become increasingly contentious. As society has become more diverse and as the glue that binds society together dissolves competition among different groups intensifies whereby the real lessons of sport shines through. Examples from disparate societies suggest that this tendency develops independently of disparities in relative wealth and (in)equality. As Francis Fukuyama observes, the biggest obstacle to achieving equality among people is not their innate difference in ability but a human striving for inequality driven by ambition. The desire to excel and gain recognition is incompatible with the idea that everyone should be equal.

A central discussion about equality relates to gender, and to this I turn next. The vast majority of people in the west agree that men and women should have the same rights and opportunities and that chromosomes should not exclude anyone from pursuing their dreams, whatever they may be. However, gender inequality is a preconditional fact of life due to innate biological differences. This is unmistakably the case in the world of sport, which is why it provides a suitable context for discussing how best to promote gender equality in areas where biology makes the sexes unequal at the outset. A radical solution, proposed by Torbjörn Tännsjö, would be to disregard the biological differences inherent in our chromosomes and let men and women compete for the same honors in sports as in all other professions. This is, effectively, to treat people equally and accept unequal outcomes. An alternative solution could be to uphold the separation of the sexes in sports but ensure that men and women are rewarded equally in their respective categories – which would be to treat them unequally to promote equal outcomes. Both alternatives will be examined, leading us to the crucial issue of equality and equal recognition in a capitalist world, namely the classic question of pay, which will be the focal point in the second half of the essay.

It is straightforward to maintain that people should be paid the same for carrying out the same task, regardless of gender, race, and ethnicity. But problems arise when it comes to determining what it means to carry out the same task. Is playing women's football the same task as playing men's football? Do two male or female footballers in the same team perform the same task? In order to determine the fairness of equal pay you must know the value of the task that is paid for. But how do you determine the value of different tasks? In capitalist society, value is decided by the market. You get what people are willing to pay for your work. That is how market competition works.

But is that fair? These complex issues are examined from various perspectives before the essay finishes by the conclusion that the ideal of human equality is unattainable in a world of competition. Now let us dive into it.

CHAPTER 1

The Concept of Fairness

The Veronica Ivy Case as Example

In 2019, the satire news website The Babylon Bee ran a story with the headline: "Motorcyclist Who Identifies as Bicyclist Sets Cycling World Record". According to this report, the new world record holder, Judd E. Banner had smashed the previous 100-mile record by more than two hours. The Babylon Bee 'reported' that, "the brave trans-vehicle rider, was allowed to race after he told league organizers he's always felt like a bicyclist in a motorcyclist's body." Banner did not think the motor gave him an inherent advantage and rebutted critics who said, "he needs to cut off his motor in order to make the competition fairer." These people were bigots, he claimed, and he was backed by the sporting body responsible which ensured that his critics "were immediately banned from professional cycle racing" (The Babylon Bee, 2019). It is hard to believe that anyone interested in sport would fail to realize that this satire was a reference to the controversial issue of transgender athletes in sport; more specifically the Canadian transgender cyclist Rachel McKinnon, who later changed her name to Veronica Ivy.

In 2012, at the age of 29, Ivy began her transition from male to female. Six years later, in 2018, she won the UCI Masters World Track Cycling Championship, a feat that caused controversy and furor. The defending champion Sarah Fader, who beat Ivy twice in time trials earlier that same week, decided to withdraw from the finals. This was Fader's way to silently protest against the rules of the International Cycling Union (UCI), which allow transwomen to compete against biological women. Fader is an experienced racing cyclist. She competed in U.S. professional road cycling from 2006 to 2015 and now, besides participating in track racing at master's level, she is also a coach. She knows what it takes for women to reach the elite level. The fact that Ivy had only been track racing for two years before she was crowned world champion cemented Fader's conviction that UCI's inclusion of transwomen in women's cycling was wrong: "It's taken some women five to eight years to get that fast and [Ivy] made these leaps and bounds in a few years. […] For her being such a beginner and being able to hit these times that took us years to hit how do you even measure that progression?" (Dreier, 2018).

Fader was not the only rival dissatisfied with UCI's decision to let Ivy take part in the event. Another of Ivy's competitors, Jennifer Wagner-Assali, could not resist the temptation to vent her frustration in a response to a photo of the winners' podium tweeted by British commentator Katie Hopkins with the withering comment: "For clarity – this was the WOMEN's world championships. I repeat. Women's. Congratulations to the brave face of silver and bronze. The world is gripped by febrile madness." In her retweet Wagner-Assali wrote: "I was the 3rd place rider. It's definitely NOT fair."

Not everyone in the competition was as critical about transwomen's inclusion as Fader and Wagner-Assali. Wagner-Assali's tweet provoked Dutch silver-medalist Carolien van Herrikhuyzen to respond in support of Ivy: "I totally disagree. No one is a transgender to steal anyone's medal. We had an honest race under UCI rules. If you compete you accept the rules, otherwise, don't compete. I can only imagine what she had to go through in her life to be where she is now. How hard it is to fit in."

The two losing rivals' feud over Ivy's eligibility brings the concept of fairness to the fore. Wagner-Assali's tweet assumes that there is some essential meaning in this concept. Accordingly, she maintains that it is unfair for transwomen to participate in women's sports no matter what the rules say. Wagner-Assali's criticism is rooted in the fact that transwomen are biological men (defined as the sex that carries one x and one y chromosome), who have had their physique altered by medical intervention to become more like the gender they identify as. Yet, before its transformation, Ivy's body was in irrevocable ways shaped by male hormones. Hence, there is reason to suppose that she holds a competitive advantage over biological women in track cycling. According to Fader, Ivy's performances are a clear indication that her gender transformation process has not eliminated this advantage. A 2020 pro-transgender athlete column in the New York Times admitted that, "some evidence suggests that residual strength and muscle mass advantages largely remain when people assigned as males at birth undergo testosterone suppression for a year" (Brassil & Longman, 2020). Later that same year, further evidence added to the suspicion that transwomen hold a significant advantage over biological women, as a new study on transgender athletes found that transwomen retain a 12% advantage in running tests even after having taking hormones for two years to suppress their testosterone. The study indicates that the International Olympic Committee guidelines regarding the transgender issue give transwomen an 'unfair competitive advantage' over biological women (Roberts, Smalley, & Ahrendt, 2021).

In contrast, Herrikhuyzen's argument is rooted in an understanding of fairness as void of innate meaning. In her view, the concept only makes sense in relation to socially constructed conventions. That is, the meaning of fairness in sport is directly linked to the rules of the specific disciplines. You only behave unfairly if you break the rules. Consequently, if rules allow transwomen to compete in the women's category, it is fair that they do so, regardless of any biologically determined advantage they may have due to their sex. The discrepancy between the two athletes' understanding of fairness was illuminated by Wagner-Assali's response to Herrikhuyzen's argument: "Just because it's a CURRENT UCI rule doesn't make it fair or right. And rules can be changed" (Stuff, 2018).

At first glance Herrikhuyzen's remark seems irrefutable. How can it be unfair for an athlete to take part in a sport that he or she is eligible to take part in according to the rules in place? What makes Herrikhuyzen's claim persuasive is that she uses the term fairness as if it were a synonym for legality, which it is not. The difference between the two concepts emerges when applied to issues outside of sports. For instance, if legislation says people of a certain skin color are not allowed to sit on certain benches, or that all people regardless of income should be taxed the same amount of money, many would probably find it cynical to dismiss questions about the fairness of such arrangements with reference to the civil and tax laws in place. Indeed, many might feel it morally justified to infringe the rules. By the same token, it is hard to imagine that Herrikhuyzen would apply the same line of reasoning if UCI decided to solve the transgender eligibility issue by making all cycling races under their auspices gender neutral.

Most people agree that it would be unfair to women if sports' governing bodies embraced the gender equality agenda and eliminated the stereotypical sex categories all together. In line with this, a 2021 Politico poll found that 46 percent of American women and 59 percent of American men somewhat or strongly support banning transgender athletes from competing in women's sports at state high schools and universities, whereas 34 percent of women and 29 percent of men were strongly or somewhat opposed to the ban (Politico, 2021). The majority's support of a ban is probably based on the assumption that transwomen hold a competitive advantage over biological women. In keeping with this, it is telling that Ivy did not rebut Wagner-Assali's claim that her participation was unfair by referring to the regulations, as Herrikhuyzen did. Instead, Ivy insisted that she did not have a competitive advantage by mentioning that Wagner-Assali had beaten her on several occasions in 2016 and 2017 before she managed to win the world championship in 2018 (Stuff, 2018). The message Ivy seemingly wanted to convey was not that the existence of gender-based physical advantages is a myth, but that hormonal sex change procedures annul the advantage transgender women had over biological women prior to their change. This was not backed by hard evidence, but Ivy could find some support for her claim in a review article, which, on the basis of the lack of scientific studies of the topic at the time, concluded that, "there is no direct or consistent research suggesting transgender female individuals (or male individuals) have an athletic advantage at any stage of their transition" (Jones, Arcelus, Bouman, & Haycraft, 2017).

Nevertheless, in 2019 Ivy defended her world champion title in even more convincing fashion during the UCI Masters World Championships in Manchester. She set a new world record in the 200 meters match sprint. Predictably, these achievements once again fueled debate about the fairness of trans-women's participation in women's sports. The question of transgender athletes' right to compete against biologically female athletes is clearly relevant in a sporting context. Here it is an issue governing bodies must negotiate and find practical solutions to. But the question is of wider interest. The controversy surrounding Ivy's eligibility illustrates how the practical world of sports can improve our vision and benefit our understanding of similar issues in society at large, where inclusion (and exclusion), diversity, equality and fair competition are increasingly subject to debate.

The Ideal of Equality

The reality of elite sport as a clearly competitive environment can be used to qualify our understanding of the competitive nature of society at large and thus of the conflicts of interest that take place inside and outside societal institutions. A mainstay in modern upbringing is the commandment to treat other people fairly, equally, and respectfully. We find these values exercised in relation to sport when athletes shake hands before and after matches, when they interrupt play so an injured opponent can get treatment, when they praise opponents' efforts in post-match interviews etc. Such gestures are being hailed as examples of true sportsmanship although it should be noted that they typically take place outside or in the margins of the sporting contest (Deleney, 2016). During the game the will to win takes precedence and with increased importance and intensity of the competition gamesmanship and even worse kinds of unfairness prevails. In the heat of the game moral values tend to fade whilst less positive character traits come to the fore and reminds us about the relationship between sport and war. As Leslie A. Howe observes:

> There are many instances of sporting malpractice and general bad behavior that can certainly contribute to such an overall strategy that might or might not contribute strict instances of gamesmanship per se, rather than something else. For example,

> fakery intended to deceive officials and gain field advantage (e.g. Rivaldo's mime during Brazil's game against Turkey at the 2002 World Cup), taking advantage of bad calls that one did not engineer (not admitting that the puck or ball was over the line), ordinary cheating (illegal equipment, doping) attempting to injure an opponent, or overloading the officials with borderline or even flagrant fouls in the knowledge that not all of them will be called... (Howe, 2004, p. 213)

In elite sport the varnish of socialization wears off and the competitive nature of humans comes to light and makes it apparent that beneath our educational ideals there is a human reality which does not conform to these ideals but in fact seems to be their opposite.

In the wake of the Second World War, the United Nations was formed with the aim of preventing future wars. One of the organization's primary purposes was to promote recognition of common rights for all human beings regardless of class, sex, and skin color. The UN's *Universal Declaration of Human Rights*, adopted in 1948, states that: "All human beings are born free and equal in dignity and rights. They are endowed with reason and conscience and should act towards one another in a spirit of brotherhood" (United Nations, 1948 art. 1). This first article of the declaration draws heavily on Enlightenment ideas. It almost echoes the first article of the *French Declaration of the Rights of Man and of the Citizen* adopted in 1789, which states that: "Men are born and remain free and equal in rights. Social distinction can be founded only on the common good" (Marquis de Lafayette, 1789). Both statements express an ideal that are widely recognized as a sound foundation for a just life in modern secular societies. As sport reminds us, they do not mirror reality, though. People are not born free and equal. From birth everyone is dependent on parents or other guardians. Some are lucky to be born into a caring and resourceful family, others may find themselves in a less fortunate environment, which makes equality illusory from the outset. Normally, people are endowed with cognitive capacities, but surely not to the same degree. Although intelligence research is a controversial topic that has not always been used for the good commonly used intelligence tests such as the Wechsler Adult Intelligence Scale reveal that cognitive abilities are not evenly distributed (Cherry, 2020; Martschenko, 2017). Some people are more gifted than others. This is inequality determined by nature. The same is true for individuals' chromosomes that control what sex the embryos evolve into and their potential for height, maximum oxygen uptake and so on.

Sport is commonly understood as a test of athletes' natural abilities and has often been used as an argument against doping in sports (Loland, 2018; T. H. Murray, 2018). Athletes can improve their innate properties to a certain level by practicing. Still, athletes are limited individually by their innate characteristics. So – sheer luck aside – despite all their efforts, less gifted athletes are doomed to fail in competition against more gifted ones that practice with the same level of commitment.

A common anti-doping argument is that the use of performance enhancing substances gives athletes an unnatural performance boost. The basis for this argument is the assumption that it is wrong if top motivated athletes use "artificial" products to overcome natural deficits. Mediocre athletes who identify as elite level athletes would be unlikely to meet much sympathy if, individually or as a pressure group, they began to campaign for the right to medical assistance allowing them to match the level of athletic performance they identify with. They could argue that the acceptance of doping would be in accordance with the ideals of fairness and human equality. Still, it is hard to imagine that this argument would win over sufficient numbers of people to prompt the doping ban to be lifted. In the world of sport, there seems to be general agreement that natural inequalities should not only be accepted but protected and celebrated (Loland, 2018; T. H. Murray, 2018).

Interestingly, in the western world recognition of the UN dictum "that all human beings are born free and equal in dignity and rights" seems to be spreading into almost all other areas. Certainly, there are still chauvinists, racists, and homophobes around, but chauvinism, racism, and homophobia have been removed from the legal framework of western societies. Homosexuality is no longer a criminal offence, Jim Crow laws have gone, and today's women have equal access to all societal privileges, which is a massive achievement, if we consider they were excluded from most of these, including the right to own property, and the right to vote, which they did not get until a little over a century ago. Equal access has been formally granted to every adult citizen in western liberal democracies regardless of race, gender, and sexual orientation. Some states have introduced affirmative action policies to bridge inequality gaps established by past discrimination. Even in cases where minority groups' interests go against core values of majority groups, it is often the interests of the latter that yield. Yet various interest groups continue to fight for improved recognition of their rights. In an attempt to show how current policy is no longer primarily about economic equality but much more about equal recognition Francis Fukuyama points to the gay rights movement:

> Take, for example, the gay marriage movement, which has spread like wildfire across the developed world in the first decades of the twenty-first century. This does have an economic aspect, having to do with rights of survivorship, inheritance, and

the like for gay or lesbian unions. However, many of those economic issues could have been and were in many cases resolved through new rules about property in civil unions. But a civil union would have had a lower status than a marriage: society would say that gay people could be together legally, but their bond would be different from that between a man and a woman. This outcome was unacceptable to millions of people who wanted their political systems to explicitly recognize the equal dignity of gays and lesbians; the ability to marry was just a marker of that equal dignity. And those opposed wanted something of the opposite: a clear affirmation of superior dignity of a heterosexual union and therefore of the traditional family. (Fukuyama, 2018, p. 19)

Fukuyama is probably right that the wish for wider societal recognition was a stronger incentive behind the campaign for acceptance of same sex marriage than the economic insecurity related to life in informal relationships. He may also be right that some of those who opposed this demand felt that traditional heterosexual relationships were of "superior dignity". But there is another important aspect that drives the opposition that he leaves untouched. In many conservative believers' minds homosexuality is a sin. According to a strict reading, Leviticus 18, 22 is incontrovertible: "You shall not lie with a male as with a woman; it is an abomination." In this light, it is unsurprising that same sex marriage with the church's blessing is blasphemy in the eyes of conservative Christians (van der Toorn, Jost, Packer, Noorbaloochi, & Van Bavel, 2017). While liberal secularists find literalist readings of the Bible outdated their Christian opponents see churches' liberal acceptance of the homosexual request as a blatant rule violation within the religious "game".

Homosexual marriages were not acknowledged anywhere in the world until in December 2000 the Netherlands became the first country to legalize same-sex marriage. Since then, a growing number of countries in the modern world have followed suit. As a result, in countries that have admitted homosexuals' legal right to same-sex marriage in city halls and churches, the sentiments of people with conservative religious convictions have been neglected. It is true that vicars in these countries can refuse to marry homosexuals, citing their religious belief. But neither they nor their congregation can prevent their places of worship being, in their eyes, profaned to accommodate liberal ideas about inclusion, the recognition of relationships and sexual practices which – according to their beliefs – are sinful. For Christian conservatives, this is not necessarily a question of personal preference, ill-will or revulsion. It is a question of faith and identity. Christian conservatives often use the Bible as a rulebook. Thus, believers' can base their objection to gay marriage on theological grounds with reference to Matthew 19, 4-5 "the Creator made them male and female ... For this reason, a man will leave his father and mother and be united to his wife and the two will become one flesh." Unwilling to concede that they may have misinterpreted the passages they refer to they can claim that those who accept gay church weddings do not play by the rules, (Gnuse, 2015). Or they can apply different tactics and protest against it bio-culturally, arguing that the purpose of marriage is to promote procreation and, since procreation requires union between male and a female, same-sex marriage is unnatural and fruitless (Ball, 2014). If such protests have fallen on deaf ears, it could be argued, the reason is that the identity of Christian conservatives is not being respected. A compromise could be that same-sex marriages were allowed to take place in town halls and other relevant places but not in churches, and with all the pomp and circumstance of a church wedding and with identical legal ramifications. Such a compromise would indicate that the political system recognizes the equal dignity of gays and lesbians while at the same time respecting the faith and identity of conservative Christians. But none of the parties seem willing to settle for a draw. And if the political system accepts, in its respect for the conservative Christian tradition, the exclusion of homosexual church weddings, it can still be accused of (allowing) discrimination against the gay population. Hence, the only way to eliminate the problem of discrimination against homosexuals is to grant them the right to be married in churches in contravention of the faith and will of the religious protesters, which in effect means that the church as a "haven" for believers has been desecrated, secularized, and thereby annulled.

From a secularist perspective this outcome seems fair. Why should the state allow churches to exclude a group of taxpayers from their services any more than a bus company, a restaurant or any other public facility? However, if we acknowledge that religion is a valuable and meaningful asset in society and accordingly accept religious considerations, the case is not so simple. Some Christian conservatives perceive any call for churches to open up to same-sex marriage as a malicious attack on the meaning of the institution and on their religion. To them state legalization of same-sex marriages in churches is humiliating and an indication of disregard of their faith. All of which only goes to prove that pursuing the ideal of equality and equal recognition is not necessarily a straight-forward matter. The conflict between the gay rights movement and the anti-gay marriage movement that Fukuyama refers to in the quote above exemplifies, first that different values, worldviews, and belief systems are not easily reconciled, and second that rights are not peacefully negotiated between people in mutual recognition of their differences but established in battles with winners and losers.

Equality and Power

As we have just seen, attempts to promote equal rights and recognition of some groups are often made at the expense of the recognition and rights of other groups. Because people subscribe to different ideologies and find different meaning in their lives, equilibrium is unattainable. Rights and recognition are not given but must be earned. Behind the admirable efforts to increase equality, there lies an unmistakable struggle for power. Interest groups and advocates of the marginalized and underprivileged often maintain that everyone deserves equal rights and recognition, and this appeal is useful as a lever in striving for these ends because it sounds intuitively right and presents a beautiful and worthy ideal.

Bishop Talbot's vision quoted in the introduction, of sport without rivalry and his advocacy of a "soul-saving" sporting attitude that put the joy of the contest over the will to win, corresponds with this ideal. This is unsurprising, because equality and recognition of the marginalized and underprivileged fit the Christian school of thought. But would such an ideal ever be possible to establish? And if so, would it be human? If we think of the kingdom of heaven, which is the prime example in western culture of an imagined place where everybody shares the same divine privileges and blissful happiness how would the order of the afterlife for the chosen ones be? Would hierarchy be eliminated, and everyone be equal? Or would God and Jesus still be around with demands of all sorts of worship from those inferiors who are admitted thanks to their efforts? Would Moses, David, Abraham, the prophets, and the disciples be given the same status as all the millions of souls only God remembers on Judgement Day? Let us assume God and Jesus had had enough of prayers and had left the scene for a penthouse paradise from which they could survey the life of the redeemed flock. What would they see? A world with no positions to jockey for, and no problems to be resolved? A world where previously intelligent, hard-working, creative, innovative, and productive people were sitting idle in a state of endless happiness without needs, concerns, desires, ambitions, conflicts, and challenges like cud-chewing animals in a fold filled with juicy grass, just jollier? An existence without sense of purpose or meaning other than patting one another on the back cheerfully shouting, "We made it!" as if they had won a world championship? And triumph even of this limited sense is hard to imagine. Because such celebration would imply memory of the challenge and awareness that their absent contemporaries of the old world that did not make it. If the chosen ones, rather than pitying, grieving and missing their family, friends and acquaintances condemned to everlasting damnation, celebrate their own salvation, it would imply that they possess feelings of pride and superiority. Their celebration would demonstrate lack of empathy with those who were relegated to the darkness, which is seldom associated with the piousness religious people usually pride themselves on. However, if memory of the losers were erased from the minds of the chosen ones during resurrection, there would be no memory of victory and thus nothing to celebrate.

This brings us back to elite sport which it has been argued represents an antithesis to Christian values (Brooks, 2012; Møller, 2010). From sport we learn that the sweet taste of victory is temporary. You may win once, but staying at the top means you must continue to train hard and do your utmost to keep your rivals at bay. If you follow Talbot's advice and stop caring whether you win or lose you will soon be lost at elite level. Complacency is a dangerous mindset. Athletes who lose their determination to maintain their position above and beyond their competitors will be overthrown by hungrier rivals willing to give what it takes to become successful.

It is consistent with the very nature of competitive sport that rivals should want to overpower their opponents and see them suffer defeat. No victory is won without loss to an opponent. Celebration of victory is celebration of superiority. The gold medal hung around the victor's neck signifies that the winner is valued more than silver and bronze medalists, not to speak of the also-rans, who are left empty-handed. Sport ruthlessly exposes the fact that equality among humans is an illusion. Even more radically, sport demonstrates that the ideal of human equality is a pipedream promoted mainly by those who would profit from its realization or by those for whom privilege and power is so entrenched that they are unable to imagine being without it. However, all things considered, to call for equality is just another strategic move in the power game that springs from the competitive nature of human life. If people gave up their privileges (in the name of equality), they would soon realize that their place and their privilege would be taken by others exploiting the vacant privileges for their own. They would not revert to the common good. As Fukuyama poignantly explains:

> Striving to be unequal comes to light in all aspects of life even in events like the Bolshevik Revolution that sought to create a society based on complete human equality. Men like Lenin, Trotsky, and Stalin were not individuals who personally strove to be merely the equals of other people: had this been the case, Lenin would never have left Samara and Stalin might well have remained a seminary student in Tbilisi. To make a revolution and create an entirely new society requires remarkable individuals with greater than usual hardness, vision, ruthlessness and

> intelligence, characteristics which all of these early Bolsheviks possessed in abundance. (Fukuyama, 1992, p. 304)

The will-to-power dynamic implied in Fukuyama's quote above is not limited to poor and highly unequal societies where real hunger is a lived experience. We also find it in relatively equal affluent societies with a homogeneous population and full democracy. In such societies the will-to-power often expresses itself within institutional frameworks as ideological conflicts. Sweden offers a thought-provoking example.

Feminism and Institutions of Higher Education in Sweden

Swedish society has been shaped by the Social Democratic Workers' Party of Sweden that have "freedom equality and solidarity" written into their party program and been in government almost uninterruptedly since 1932. The Swedish government proudly presents itself as "the first feminist government in the world". This means, among other things, that

> a gender equality perspective is brought into policy-making on a broad front, both nationally and internationally. Women and men must have the same power to shape society and their own lives. This is a matter of democracy and justice. (Government Offices of Sweden, 2019)

These are not empty words. Gender equality has been high on the agenda in Sweden for decades. In 1998, the Swedish Secretariat for Gender Research (SSGR) was designated to coordinate gender equality initiatives and gender research in all institutions of higher education in the country. In 2002, presumably to advance the gender equality agenda, the Swedish government publicly announced that gender is a social construction. Indeed, a contested philosophical theory was adopted by the state as established truth. Swedish language makes no distinction between "sex" and "gender". It is true that gender research translates "genusforskning" not "könnsforskning" but in everyday usage sex and gender are covered by the same term "könn", which makes the government's announcement sound even more radical than it does in English. No matter whether one agrees with the Swedish government's understanding of "könn" or not, its ambition to oppose sex discrimination and secure equal opportunities and a level playing field for both sexes is laudable. In order to achieve this goal, the government worked out a directive in 2015, which emphasized the need to ensure that universities are safe, just, and pleasant working places for all, regardless of sex, race, and sexual orientation. This includes just distribution of research funds, tenure and so forth.

The implementation of this radical egalitarian directive was entrusted the SSGR. Education researcher Anna-Karin Wyndhamn was appointed to help roll out the accreditation process. Gender equality was a topic Wyndhamn was passionate about. She began her appointment at SSGR full of clear-eyed optimism but after a while she became skeptical. She noticed that the prevailing understanding in the institution was that sex differences did not exist and that the use of the nouns, "men" and "women", and the pronouns, "him" and "her", was frowned upon. What troubled Wyndhamn was not so much that all her colleagues thought that there were no essential differences between the sexes but that this understanding had become a doctrine within the secretariat, which apparently everyone agreed should be imposed on all institutions under their jurisdiction. Equipped with the necessary governmental authority, SSGR employees evaluated the universities' gender equality initiatives, and they did not take this task lightly. According to Wyndhamn, who – uncomfortable with the ideological approach – soon began to record the secretariat's activism, SSGR did not just read action plans to see if they met the criteria for gender equality. That is, if universities played by the rules. In authoritarian fashion they edited the various universities' action plans and introduced buzzwords such as "intersectional theory," "norm criticism" and "power relations analyses". The autonomy of the universities was not respected. If a university proposed launching an internal investigation to determine the extent of the gender equality problem, SSGR's response was that investigations were unnecessary because they were already familiar with the situation. The "assistance" the universities received from the secretariat was, in reality, a directive. Unprepared for the assault on their managerial rights, university management chose to dance to the tune of the powerful SSGR and be certified, irrespective of staff members' protests. Wyndhamn mentions the example of a university hospital that was supposed to become LGBT-certified. All staff members were obliged to participate in mandatory seminars. During the seminars, many of the doctors defended their territory. They posed critical questions and asked for evidence underpinning the information presented to them. This critical approach was not welcomed by the hospital's project managers, because it had made the external presenters at the seminar feel uncomfortable and unwilling to return, so the LGBT-certificate was hanging by a tread. To solve the problem, the project managers decided to send out a brief instruction by SMS to the doctors involved: "Stop asking critical questions. Sit still and listen" (Arpi & Wyndhamn, 2020, p. 66). A message that went directly against the very *raison d'être* of a university.

What makes this Swedish example particularly valuable is that it demonstrates how a relatively small power base can be exploited by strong-minded people with a course. SSGR's role was to monitor whether Swedish institutions of higher education lived up to the government's gender equality agenda. Yet the secretariat seized this opportunity to use this role to impose its own feminist ideology on universities – an ideology that, according to Wyndhamn and Arpi, is indistinguishable from the program of the party Feminist Initiative, which received a mere 0.46 percent of the votes at the general election in 2018.

Clearly, universities are themselves powerful institutions. They could have chosen to actively resist the secretariat's interference in their affairs. But universities are also old institutions that take their role as autonomous authorities for granted. Their centuries-old status has made them complacent and less resistant to attacks on their autonomy. They do not have the same appetite for defending their territory when it is attacked as those who hold new convictions and want to see change do. Despite their powerful status as truth-seeking knowledge-producing scientific institutions, they are vulnerable. Scandinavian universities are state funded. This financial dependence further limits the institutions' willingness to exert resistance. They are all too aware that there are risks involved in attracting negative attention by opposing a controlling body designated by the government to monitor their activities, even if this body goes beyond its remit. As Helen Pluckrose and James Lindsay observe:

> University administrators are as sensitive to public relations as corporate executives, though the political environment in which they navigate is quite different (especially for public universities, which are at the direct mercy of elected politicians). This produces a complex set of pressures on university administra-

> tors, in which the protection of academic freedom is frequently not the highest priority. (Pluckrose & Lindsay, 2021, p. 221)

This may explain why university managements across Sweden rolled over instead of opposing the strong-willed secretariat.

The Ideal of Gender Equality

Given the all-encompassing competitiveness that pervades human life, it may be puzzling that gender equality has become a political priority. Not only does gender equality find support in Sweden and all other western societies. It has global backing, as attested by the solidarity movement for gender equality, HeForShe, launched in 2014 by the UN. Given the competitive nature of life, what is even more mysterious is that gender equality has been achieved in numerous domains, albeit mostly in the western world, with many influential men supporting women's fight for equality. It could have been expected that the sex in possession of the power and means to defend the status quo would do so to protect their dominant position. The conundrum does have an explanation, however. First, women have fought fiercely for the rights they have won. Suffragettes like Emily Wilding Davison sacrificed their lives for the cause (Collette, 2013). Second, hitherto gender equality has not been achieved at the expense of men in power. On the contrary. Women's entry into the labor market was good for the economy. It increased both the gross domestic product and the material wealth of families, which, in turn, benefitted men and women alike (Ostry, Alvarez, Espinoza, & Papageorgiou, 2018). And third, women's inclusion in the workforce was a welcome addition that strengthened a nation's competitiveness.

It should be noted, however, that gender equality in terms of rights and equal opportunities are not equivalent to equality of outcome. Hence there is ongoing discussion as to whether gender equality has indeed been achieved, even in the Nordic countries where gender parity is most advanced. The above-mentioned SS-GR's policing of Swedish universities' gender equality initiatives shows that at least some feminists still think that this is not the case. The core of this debate has to do with different understandings of the concept of gender equality. Some think that equality is reached when women have the same rights and access to the same career opportunities as men. Others argue that gender equality does not exist if women are not on a par with men in all influential and high-status positions in society. For instance, although men and women have the same right to vote and both are free to pursue political careers with the same ambition, women do not hold half of the seats in parliament in any of the developed countries, although Sweden is coming close at 47.3 percent (Inter-Parliamentary Union, 2019). So, seen from the perspective of equal representation, gender equality has not been achieved by women's right to vote and to pursue a political career. Some suggest, therefore, that quota systems that ensure equal representation must be introduced if gender equality is ever to be achieved. Sweden's almost equal representation is, in part, the result of voluntary party quotas. This indicates that quotas are the way forward.

Yet, those who argue in favor of equal opportunity rather than equal representation usually oppose gender quotas, arguing that if more men than women commit to politics and each sex has only half of the seats to aim for, quotas make it relatively easier for women to get elected. In other words, quotas give women an advantage. Those in favor of quotas justify such affirmative action with reference to historical discrimination against women that has cemented a structure of male dominance, which continues to suppress women and makes it harder for them to reach desirable positions in competition with men. From this perspective, quotas are a means to level out an uneven playing field (Bennett, 2014). The opponents, in contrast, argue that removal of all formal obstacles for women's active participation in society is what matters. Given free access, talented and motivated women will slowly but surely achieve the positions they are qualified for to the same extent as men. Conversely, they warn that initiatives to force through equal representation have adverse effects. If less qualified women are promoted at the expense of more qualified men in any given institution, this will, all else being equal, decrease the quality of the work of that institution (Bennett, 2014). Furthermore, the introduction of quota systems implies that women's achievements are second-rate, which from a gender equality perspective seems counter-productive.

The discussion about equality of opportunity versus equality of outcome shows that among people who agree about the value of gender equality and aim to achieve it, there is still no consensus about the best way forward. What some see as a short-cut to equality others see as steps towards a new kind of inequality. In sport, we find a lens that allows us clearly to see why it is so difficult to find common ground on the issue of gender equality.

The Challenge of Ideals

So far, I have outlined the all-encompassing impact of competition on human life and how it both works to promote equality between people and to create inequality between people. At the same time, I have shown that the liberal ideal of fairness is hard, if not impossible, to reconcile with the competitive nature of life even when it comes to negotiations of the issues of fairness and equality.

In sport the ideal of fairness and equality is manifest in the regulations which are the same for all participants. If differences in physical size and strength cause contests to turn visibly unfair, athletes are separated by age, weight, or gender. As hard as the regulating bodies try to organize sports in a fair manner, complete equality is impossible to achieve. Hence a reasonable level of fairness must be negotiated. Recent debates about trans-athletes' eligibility in competitive sports —exemplified by the Veronica Ivy case— have put the issue of fairness in sport at the forefront. Those debates have exposed both the difficulties in establishing what fair competition involves and which consideration should take precedence: transwomen's chance to compete in the sex category they identify as or the protection of women's sport as a category exclusively for biologically born females. Both viewpoints have merit, and although there surely are personal interests at play, advocates on both sides argue based on what they feel is fair. Unfortunately, it is impossible to reach a compromise that satisfies people in both camps because you simply cannot include and exclude trans-gender athletes from women's sport at the same time. One of the parties will always feel treated unfairly.

The core of the problem is humans' need for recognition, which has been amplified since the evolvement of an anti-authoritarian youth culture in the 1960s that opposed conformity in favor of expressive individualism. The struggle for recognition does not only pertain to sports but is in fact universal. And the problem of recognition is not easily solved in areas where in principle mutual recognition should be possible because of human ambition which as Fukuyama notes involves striving to become unequal. The will to prove yourself better than your opponent is inconsistent with the ideal of equality. The Swedish example bore witness to the fact that human ambition and struggle to gain recognition and move up the human hierarchy is not limited to sport but permeates human life even in one of the most equal societies in the world. So, it may be too optimistic to believe that the equalizing power of globalization will result in a decrease in different forms of conflict and violence. As philosopher Jon Stewart observes some forms of violence have actually increased.

> Instead of globalization leading to greater cross-cultural dialogue and understanding, it seems to have prompted confrontation by bringing together individuals from different cultures and religious traditions in ways that people were not prepared for. This has in many cases subsequently led to aggression and conflict. There is a broad consensus that one of the great problems confronting the world today in the 21st century is that of cultural and religious conflict that leads to violence. (Stewart, 2018, p. 467)

This sad fact should not surprise people familiar with the history of the 1908 Olympics and bishop Talbot's reaction to the international rivalry he witnessed during that event. Humans' competitive nature and will to dominate are very evident in elite sport after all. However, that those human characteristics also permeate institutions that aim toward equality and inclusion may be unexpected. The example of the Swedish higher education system under the auspices of the Swedish Secretariat for Gender Research proves this to be the case and bears witness to the potency of using sport as a lens to analyze what is going on in society in general.

The examples given hitherto reflect the competitive —rather than mutually agreeing— nature of our society despite its commitment to the liberal value of equality, particularly in the

Western world that controls large parts of sport. In the rest of this essay, I will focus solely on sports to demonstrate why it is essentially impossible to negotiate a fair and equal system with mutual recognition. It is my hope that it will be possible to see how this analysis can contribute to our understanding of related issues outside of the sporting context.

CHAPTER 2

Rights

The Right to Take Part

The vast majority of sports were invented by males. Women were excluded from participation in sports for years. Women's weaker physical constitution was often used as an explanation for their exclusion and as documented by historian Allen Guttmann, women were held back due to their social and economic role in society. Women were defined first and foremost as mothers, cooks and homemakers (Guttmann, 1991). Women's fight for recognition as athletes was also a dimension in the women's liberation. The efforts of women to defy their exclusion from sport and the joys and health benefits associated with it are praiseworthy. But they came at a price. The factual evidence made available by the inclusion of women in sport flatly contradicts what some radical feminists have claimed ever since the French philosopher Simone de Beauvoir made her inspirational statement that "one is not born, but rather becomes, a woman" (Beauvoir, 2010, p. 283), namely that experienced differences between male and female are socially constructed. The naked truth is that, statistically, men run faster, jump higher, and are stronger than women. Unsurprisingly, then, women do not stand much of a chance in sports where these are crucial components, which they are in most sports. The biological difference between the sexes makes gender equality in sports a problematic and controversial pursuit. Philosophers who have tried to solve this problem have come up with contrasting solutions.

The Swedish philosopher Torbjörn Tännsjö, for instance, criticizes the division of the sexes in sports. Within this societal arena, sexual discrimination is simply taken for granted. The reason for separating the sexes in sports is evidently based on the observation that on average men perform better than women. But this argument is objectionable according to Tännsjö:

> First of all, this putative fact, that women perform less well than men, is hard to ascertain beyond reasonable doubt. Perhaps this is a mere statistical accident. Perhaps it is due to socially constructed gender differences rather than biological sexual differences and, hence, could be abolished. And even if the statistical correlation is due to biological sexual differences ... and even if it has a law-like character, it is still only a statistical difference. It is only indirectly, then, that sex is relevant to the outcome of a fair competition. It is relevant in the sense that it predisposes, statistically, for more or less of a certain characteristic, crucial to performing well in a certain sport. But then, if we should discriminate at all, it should be in terms of this characteristic itself and not in terms of sex. (Tännsjö, 2007, p. 349)

Tännsjö's objection poses a particular challenge to people who draw upon social constructivist ideas in their quest for gender equality, precisely because he accommodates these ideas. If differences in men and women's average performances are results of social constructions unfavorable to women, it would go against the gender equality cause to uphold the separation of the sexes in sports. The reason is that gender separation preserves the (mis)conception of women as subordinate to men. And things do not get much better, if we discard the strong social constructivist position and acknowledge that there are some biologically differences between the sexes that influence their respective performance abilities, because these differences are also merely average and statistical. As Tännsjö notes, there are also biological differences within the sexes that to a large extent determine athletic performance ability. Given this, biological differences between the sexes do not justify sex segregation in sport either. Basketball is a sport well suited to illustrate this. In contrast to rugby, basketball does not allow the use of physical force in defense. Also, precision rather than strength is required to score points. Thus, the most advantageous feature in basketball is not strength but height. This is underlined by the fact that in the history of the National Basketball Association (NBA) only 25 players out of approximately 3,000 players have been 5 ft 9 in (175 cm) or shorter, and all of these, barring one, played in the position of point guard (Stathead.com, 2011). It is true that women on average are shorter than men, but the Women's National Basketball Association (WNBA) also includes very tall women. The tallest ever being the Pole, Malgorzata (Margo) Dydek at 7ft 2in (218 cm), who retired in 2008 (Acedera, 2017). So, according to Tännsjö, from an equal opportunity point of view it would be more relevant to distinguish between tall and short players than between male and female ones.

An initiative to change basketball to a mixed-sex sport by merging the National Basketball Association (NBA) and Women's National Basketball Association (WNBA), thereby replacing gender segregation with height-based division of players would doubtless bring new problems of fairness and equality to the fore. What should be the minimum height for playing in the tall players TNBA? 6.0, 6.4, or 6.5 feet? If the latter was chosen as the cut-off point, Michael Jordan in his day would have been demoted to the smaller players SNBA. Should TNBA be open to players from the SNBA if they were good enough, the same way as boxers can challenge upwards in the weight categories but not downwards? Would two separate height categories suffice? Or should there be a league per six, four, or two inches, interval in order to minimize the height advantage? Such divisions would clearly benefit short players, who would no longer be restricted to play the position of point guard at elite level. More leagues would give many more players a chance to be drafted in, which would be another benefit from an equality of opportunity perspective. The crucial question is, however, whether there would be sufficient interest in mixed-sex basketball leagues to maintain the tournaments' profitability. The chances of basketball remaining a profitable business would naturally decrease in proportion to the number of leagues deemed necessary to minimize the height advantage. These concerns aside, even if it were possible to reduce the advantage of height in basketball to a minimum, the problem of equality and fairness would still not have been solved. With the advantage of height removed, the importance of strength and speed would grow, and this would still favor men across all the basketball leagues in the same way men are favored in all other sports where strength and speed are crucial factors. Once again, there would be those asking whether women stood a fair chance of success if they had to compete against men or whether it would be better to keep the sexes separated when the various height leagues removed tall women's advantage over shorter men, which brings us back to square one.

In sport, there will always be some body types that are more fitting than others. The small-framed, long-limbed ectomorph body shape will typically be better suited to long distance running than both the muscular broad-shouldered mesomorph, who is better suited for decathlon, and the stocky endomorph, whose lower center of gravity is advantageous in weightlifting. It should be noted that, although as a general rule ectomorph, mesomorph, and endomorph men would do better in sport than women with the same body type, this is not true in all sports. Women are generally more flexible than men which gives them an advantage in some gymnastics disciplines and in synchronized swimming. Their lighter body weight should also be an advantage in equestrian sports, where they compete alongside men. Some extraordinary ultra-endurance sports achievements in which women have won by large margins over men suggest that, physically and perhaps mentally, women are better suited for ultra-sports than men. The more grueling the challenge, the greater the advantage of the female body (S. Williams, 2019). Since sports never offer every *body* the same chance of success Tännsjö's proposal to eliminate discrimination in sport by making unisex the norm may be the fairest solution after all.

There are also other than biological factors that create uneven chances of success in disparate sports. For example, Norwegian men and women who have been brought up in a milieu where Nordic skiing is ingrained in the culture will both hold a significant advantage in cross-country skiing over Dutch men, who have been brought up in a country with no hills and seldom snow but who in adolescence get attracted to this sport. The Dutchmen may be physically stronger than the Norwegian athletes, but if they are not born with an exceptional flair for skiing, the Norwegian athletes' superior technique will most certainly leave the Dutchmen with little chance of winning. If discrimination shall take place at all, therefore, it could be argued that athletes' sports traditions and geographical location would be equally or more relevant criteria to impose. The problems associated with the gender separation currently in place would, surely, be matched by alternative ways to distinguish between athletes designed to give them a fair chance of winning. But this only strengthens the argument for indiscriminate unisex sport. At least it allows all people of all kinds to participate in the sport that appeals most to them, which usually will be those where they have the greatest chance of success.

The Right to the Same Privileges

This consequence is probably the reason why few of those in favor of gender equality are, like Tännsjö, willing to jettison gender segregation in sport. Jane English, for instance, a pioneer of feminist sports philosophy, does not agree that the introduction of indiscriminate unisex sports would be a fair solution to the fairness problem in sport. Nothing in her writing suggests that she finds any alternative groupings appealing either. She acknowledges that some males are disadvantaged in some sports due to their body composition and that it could be justified – on the grounds that differences in strength and size are only statistical – to allow these less able males a chance to qualify for teams currently reserved for females. Nevertheless, she is not willing to sacrifice gender segregated sports in favor of alternative segregation systems based on bodily features and abilities. She accepts that unisex competitions could be fair in sports such as dressage (where unisex competitions are already the norm), diving, freestyle skiing, shooting, and car racing, where sex differences are negligible if not entirely irrelevant. She is also not against the idea of inventing new disciplines or modifying old ones to increase the number of sports in which men and women can compete jointly. English even recognizes that there are sports in which women hold a natural advantage due to their body composition. An obvious example is rhythmic gymnastics. English mentions ballet, synchronized swimming, and the balance beam, the latter being "perhaps the most extreme example of a sport favoring women's natural skill" since "small size, flexibility and low center of gravity combine to give women a kind of natural hegemony that men enjoy in football" (English, 2007, p. 307). She argues that, since women have been virtually excluded from sports until the last century, it is unsurprising that few sports have been devised that discriminate in favor of the female physique, implying that sports that favor women could be expected to grow in the future. But she does not discuss the prospect of more sports designed to favor women, which is a shame because this scenario opens another interesting perspective on the gender equality issue.

It is usually the case that people take up those sports (and other hobbies) for which they have a flair, whereas they avoid sports (and hobbies) they are not suited for. So, if sports were being invented that favored the female physique, predictably many women would find these sports appealing whereas men would stick with the sports that suit them better. Yet, to the best of my knowledge, not a single person has ever publicly complained that most sports favor the male physique and called for the invention of sports in which men would be disadvantaged. Nobody, apparently, is interested in gender equality when it comes to levelling out the excessive proportion of sports that favor the male physique. A possible explanation for this could be that it would be almost impossible to design a diverse group of sports that would favor women over men. If flexibility, smallness, and low center of gravity, as English implies, are the features that give women an advantage on the balance beam (and in rhythmic gymnastics), and if all these elements must be central in a sport to favor women, the creative possibilities are indeed limited. But there is another likely explanation for the absence of complaints that only a few sports have been developed that suit women better than men or, indeed, of people who attempt to counter this disparity by designing new sports. Inventions of sports favorable to women would necessarily emphasize gender differences and stereotypes at a time in history where such differences and stereotypes are disallowed. In this day and age, the idea that there may be significant differences between men and women is opposed, at least by some feminist academics, as the Swedish example above demonstrates, almost as fiercely as the idea that there are essential differences between black, yellow, red, and white people, which in colonial times was accepted as common sense. The problem for those who deny significant gender differences is that these differences remain in sports regardless of directives to the contrary. Few pro-feminists claim, like Tännsjö, that the differences that appear in sports are results of cultural and social constructions.

One reason for the absence of such claims is that their logical consequence is to work towards cultural change by tearing down the wall that separates the sexes in sports and let them compete against one another. According to the constructivist theory, this would mean that women would face stronger opposition and as a result raise their level until, eventually, they would be on a par with the men. Most advocates of gender equality do not have sufficient faith in the social construction theory to work for this 'solution', probably because they realize that it would prove counter-productive in the real world. Hence, they stick – albeit tacitly – to an essentialist understanding of the gender differences in sports and prefer alternative approaches to gender equality. Feminists' acknowledgement of the biological sex difference in terms of strength, whereby they concede that women are physically weaker than men, give them a stronger hand to play. Being the physically weaker sex, women need to have special consideration, as implied in English's reasoning.

According to English, gender equality is not merely a question of men and women's equal right to take part in the same sports. If, for instance, all tennis tournaments were unisex, even women with a sublime technique would barely stand a chance of success because of the dominant male physique. Seen in this light, English argues that formal equality between the sexes regarding access and opportunity is insufficient to create real gender equality. Because of the irrefutable differences in size and strength, men will inevitably have an advantage over women in most unisex sports – at least if we think of the sports the Olympic Games currently comprise. Hence women will not see many winners with whom they can identify. Accordingly, they will not find many motivational role models in Olympic sports. "So, far from being necessary for equal opportunity, sex-blindness can actually decrease it", English asserts (English, 2007, p. 304). Her reason for wanting to maintain segregation based on sex rather than other relevant features is not that integration would be a problem for the individual women who were to be beaten by men. Her main argument is that the outcome would be harmful to women in general:

> When there are virtually no female athletic stars, or when women receive much less prize money than men do, this is damaging to the self-respect of all women ... If women do not attain roughly equal fame and fortune in sports, it leads both men and women to think of women as naturally inferior. Thus, it is not a right of women tennis stars to the scarce benefits, but rather a right of all women to self-respect that justifies their demand for equal press coverage and prize money. (English, 2007, p. 305)

It is easy to sympathize with English's concern for women's self-respect. Having said that, aspects of her reasoning are not self-evident, and its implications are, when one thinks about it, rather controversial. First, if it is true that gender equality in sport would decrease as a result of equal access for all, without taking sex differences into account, the question arises as to why this would be the case. Surely, role models often inspire children and adolescents to take up sports. The feats of the two great American cyclists Greg LeMond and Lance Armstrong at the Tour de France have undoubtedly, in their day, motivated many American youngsters to take up cycling. Although neither of them is a woman, there is reason to believe that the American cycling heroes' much-celebrated achievements may have inspired some American girls to do likewise. At any rate, since LeMond and Armstrong dominated the cycling world's most famous stage race, the number of American bicycle owners have been on the rise and notably, in 2012, 60 percent of American bicycle owners in the 18 to 27 years age group were women (Kohout, 2013). Why, we have to ask, in a gender-neutral world, would girls need to find their role models in their own sex? If girls need female role models to be motivated for sports, one may wonder how women got motivated for sports in the first place. Yet, women have found their way into many sports that were originally exclusively male domains such as boxing, wrestling, rugby, football, and soccer.

Second, English claims that women's self-respect will be damaged if there are no female stars or if those female stars who are in sports only get a fraction of the available prize money. But these assumptions are backed by no evidence. Even if women were totally absent from the world of sports, it is unclear why this should harm women's self-respect per se. If true, we might expect women's self-respect to be totally wrecked given all the areas in which they are not equally represented and rewarded. The number of female rock bands, female conductors of classical music, female chefs at restaurants with Michelin stars, female astronauts, not to mention female multi-billionaires is paltry in comparison with their male counterparts. Fortunately, self-respect is not determined externally by other people's achievements and successes. Self-respect pertains to people's ability to come to terms with who and what they are, to put up with their limitations and shortcomings, and to find satisfaction in their actual capabilities. There are plenty of men and women who are not the least interested in sport. It is hard to imagine that any of these individual's self-respect would be in the least affected, positively or negatively, by the (lack of) gender representation in any given sport. So English's assumption that gender representation affects non-participants' self-respect must, if true at all, be limited to those men and women who hold an interest in sports.

Now, if we think of female spectators who passionately follow the English Premier League in an imagined world where no female football tournament existed, why should this in any way be damaging to these women's self-respect? They have voluntarily taken interest in football; they root for a team and feel as strongly as any man the joy and dejection when "their" team is winning or losing. How should a woman's passion for male football erode her self-respect more than it erodes that of any male who had the advantage of being born the gender that allowed him to play professional football but failed due to his physical features or his lack of talent? Of course, if women themselves wanted to play and were denied this with reference to their gender, such gender-based discrimination could potentially be harmful to these women's self-respect. But not necessarily. It could also make them rebel, in self-respect, against the (imagined) order of things. In fact, it was those confident women who refused to accept women's exclusion from sports who began the fight for the acceptance of women's participation. One of these pioneers, Kathrine Switzer, entered the Boston Marathon in 1967 having signed in as a gender-neutral K.V. Switzer because it was prohibited for women to participate. She bravely made it to the finishing line despite an official's attempt to force her out of the race two miles in. By registering for the race, Switzer challenged the exclusion of women from it. It could be argued, then, that as long as women in all but a few sports are kept in separate categories, those women who have fought for women's right to participate in sports competitions have only half-succeeded.

This was the issue when, in 1973, Billie Jean King, one of the world's best female tennis players at the time, beat the 55-year-old Bobby Riggs who had publicly belittled women's tennis by stating that the female game was inferior to men's tennis and that, although he had retired as a tennis player 22 years ago, he still could beat any of the female top players. King's victory, in the match that became known as "the battle of the sexes" boosted the recognition of women's tennis. King, however, did not use her victory to promote unisex tennis, which was probably a wise decision as there is a world of difference between beating a retired unfit 55-year-old male tennis player and competing against the male elite in unisex tournaments. Aware that it would be devastating for her cause if she lost, King had declined Riggs challenge at first. What forced King to take up the gauntlet was that her rival, Margaret Court, lured by the prize money, had accepted Riggs' challenge and lost. Court, who was number one on the women's world ranking list at the time and had won 89 of her previous 92 matches, lost the match 6-2, 6-1 in just 57 minutes (Drucker, 2021). The match became known as "the Mothers' Day massacre". "The battle of the sexes" was played best of five sets. King won in three straight sets, but it was no massacre. The match ended 6-4, 6-3, 6-3 after Riggs had made a series of unforced errors, and "rumors circulated that Riggs – who were said to have a large gambling debt to the Mafia […] –threw the match in order to erase his debt to the mob" (Augustyn, Invalid Date). Whatever the truth of the matter, King's victory gave a boost to her gender equality agenda, and shortly after she founded the Women's Tennis Association (WTA) for the purpose of pushing for prize money parity. Although it has not been implemented across all tennis tournaments 34 years down the road, this goal was eventually achieved at the grand slam level when Wimbledon finally agreed to equal pay in 2007 (Cambers, 2018).

Originally King had hoped to form an all-players' union, but this idea, she says, was shot down, and she does not believe a joint organization will ever be established: "I don't see it," she says. "The guys don't want to share. They think we're in the way: 'Get out of here.' They don't think we have any clout" (Cambers, 2018). If it was true that female tennis players did not have any influence, as King asserts is the general perception of male players, it would be hard to understand how women achieved pay parity at grand slam level. So, perhaps the reason for male tennis players unwillingness to join forces with the female players could be slightly different, namely that negotiation power in contractual matters depends on market value. It would be naïve to think that women have achieved pay parity simply because, when the Women's Tennis Association brought the topic up, the tournament organizers suddenly realized it was unjust to pay women less than men. The logic of the market is that you pay what you have to pay for a commodity or a service. Buyers will tend to negotiate a price as low as possible, whereas sellers seek to get as much as they possibly can. Accordingly, as long as women accepted playing for less than men, it would be foolish of the organizers to reduce their profit by paying them more. The formation of the WTA strengthened the female players' negotiating power. When the female tennis players united, the organizers were forced to reconsider the deal. The men, for their part, had formed the men's Association of Tennis Professionals (ATP) in September 1972. If the male players had assessed that their deal could be further improved by forming a union with the female players, they would probably have done so. King was most likely correct when she said that the guys did not want to share. This can be interpreted as male chauvinism. On the other hand, as implied in King's wording, if men and women were supposed to share the purse, women would get more while the men would get less. So, from a financial point of view, the male players had little incentive to join forces. This invites the question: Was it unfair of the male players to reject the proposal of an all-players union that would work for pay parity at their expense?

CHAPTER 3

Equal Pay

The Fairness of Equal Pay

According to the ideal expressed in the abovementioned declarations of human rights, people are equal in dignity and rights and should act towards one another in a spirit of brotherhood. Presumably, brothers and sisters should share equitably. Not always 50/50 maybe, but fairly. The idea of fair distribution finds expression in the *French Declaration on the Rights of Man and of the Citizen*: "Social distinction can be founded only on the common good," and again in John Rawls' *A Theory of Justice* (1971), in which he argues that inequality is only justifiable so long as it is to the greatest benefit of the least advantaged in society. From Rawls' egalitarian point of view, the only justification for income differences is that this difference results in the least advantaged being better off than they would have been if all had the same. Rawls presents us with an intuitive test of fairness. People must consider what distribution they would prefer, if they were to make their choice behind a "veil of ignorance." In this "original position",

> no one knows his place in society, his class position or social status, nor does he know his fortune in the distribution of natural assets and abilities, his intelligence, strength and the like. […] The persons in the original position have no information

> as to which generation they belong. These broader restrictions are appropriate in part because questions of social justice arise between generations as well as within them, for example, the question of the appropriate capital savings and of the conservation of natural resources and the environment of nature. There is also, theoretically anyway, the question of a reasonable genetic policy. In these cases, too, in order to carry through the idea of the original position, the parties must not know the contingencies that set them in opposition. They must choose principles the consequences of which they are prepared to live with whatever generation they turn out to belong to. (Rawls, 1971, p. 137)

It seems intuitively correct that most would opt for a fairly, if not completely, even distribution if they were to make a decision under these conditions. Hence, from a Rawlsian perspective – if we look at the situation as an isolated case – it is safe to say that the male players' rejection of a joint union was unfair in so far as the reason for the rejection was that they wanted to negotiate a better deal for themselves. However, if we take a broader look at the situation Rawls is less suited to decide the case. Clearly, according to Rawls, women are entitled to the same share as men. But Rawls' theory pertains to everybody. If, for considerations of fairness, male and female elite tennis players were entitled to roughly the same income, this would also apply to para-tennis players, second-rate players, even to people unable to carry a tennis racket. Because Rawls' assumption is that, if people were deciding on distribution without knowing whether they themselves would be born male or female, skilled or unskilled, able-bodied or disabled, it is unlikely that they would decide that biologically disadvantaged people should have less than the biologically advantaged. Put differently, if it was decided that the life income of any person, tennis player or not, should be approximately the same, players' unions would be redundant because the principles of distribution was pre-ordained and prize money limited to symbolic amounts. In this scenario, the possibility of making a living from sport is not removed. But professional sports would either be de-coupled from market forces, or sports stars would be so heavily taxed that the conspicuous consumption associated with elite sports' upper echelons would be impossible to maintain.

Some might find these consequences fully acceptable. Admittedly, from a fairness point of view it is hard to defend the idea that an individual school dropout with no formal qualifications is suddenly offered a fortune to pursue a hobby because he or she is good at it. Particularly when compared to individuals with a different skills-set who have diligently spent time and effort learning a craft or becoming a teacher but must settle for salaries that do not allow them to earn in a lifetime what high-earning sportspeople make in a year. What is more useful, building houses for people and educating their children or throwing a brown ball into a basket to entertain them? Viewed this way, the valuation of different occupations appears bizarre. There is a whole range of diverse everyday tasks that must be carried out for society to work. From the viewpoint of fairness, each contribution to society ought to count the same. The problem with this equity principle is that it is ineffective. Because most jobs are not overly fulfilling, it is hardly surprising, that without pecuniary incentives people are reluctant to make an extra effort. This impedes societal progress and prosperity. That is why Rawls allows for some degree of inequality when he writes that "the higher expectations of those better situated are just if and only if they work as part of a scheme which improves the expectations of the least advantaged members of society" (Rawls, 1971, p. 75). Rawls understands that strict equal distribution would reduce people's motivation to exert themselves and that this would stunt growth and leave everybody less well-off. While Rawls clearly understands the necessity of a certain degree of inequality, it is unclear how an acceptable degree of inequality should be determined, let alone how the principle should be turned into practice. Rawls' theory implies, rather paradoxically, that if one percent of the population make a billion dollars above average, the resulting inequality is justified so long as the dealings of this select group of industrious people increase the income of the remaining 99 percent by a dollar or two. On the other hand, should 99 percent of the population manage to increase their income by ten dollars the resulting inequality would be unjust if it adversely effected the poorest one percent of the population, who were left with a reduced income of 25 cent. These examples show that pay parity and equal distribution of goods – as noble as these objectives are in principle – are impossible to translate into workable practices in the real world.

The market economy – for all its flaws – is better suited to secure a distribution of goods that motivates people for work and stimulates creativity and entrepreneurship. Even though it may, at first glance, seem unjust that one entrepreneurial person makes billions while his employees struggle to make ends meet, solid arguments as to why this is unjust are hard to come by. The problem of just distribution was famously addressed by Robert Nozick in *Anarchy, State and Utopia* (1974), where he launches a critique of Rawls' theory. Nozick accepts that a state can decide that its citizens should be entitled to the same amount of money regardless of occupation. But the introduction of an equal pay law would not solve the problem of just distribution if the state did not at the same time make laws that regulated how its citizens could spend their money. The ideal situation where everybody has the same starts to deteriorate as soon as spending begins. If one prefers to spend while another prefers to save, there will soon be a substantial difference in their holdings. Nozick asks us to consider a situation in which the much in demand basketball player Wilt Chamberlain, during contract negotiations as a free agent, demands that every spectator who comes to watch him play must put 25 cents in a box with his name on it. When the season is over one million spectators have voluntarily paid 25 cents to watch him play. They have enjoyed watching him and he had enjoyed playing in front of them. The problem of course is that now Chamberlain has $ 250,000 more than every one of the spectators. All involved knew the deal in advance so how can the resulting inequality be unjust? Nozick defuses the immediate objection, that Chamberlain is not entitled to earn this money in the first place since parity means that everybody must be paid the same regardless of occupation, by adding:

> To cut of objections irrelevant here, we might imagine the exchanges occurring in a socialist society after hours. After playing whatever basketball he does in his daily work, or doing whatever daily work he does, Wilt Chamberlain decides to put in overtime to earn additional money. (Nozick, 1974, p. 162)

The point Nozick makes is that due to the dynamics of human trade and interactions, inequality inevitably develops if the state does not constantly intervene in people's lives by taxing both their savings and the money earned doing overtime, and hand the collected amount back to the needy, who have meanwhile spent all their money. Under such circumstances, there would be no incentive to work extra or to save money to invest, and this would have detrimental consequences for the economy. As if this was not bad enough, the idealistic redistribution from frugal hoarders to wasteful squanderers is also unfair given that everyone had the same at the start.

Although the principle of (almost) equal distribution as presented by Rawls is appealing, the adverse effects of it are so serious that it is unsurprising that it has not been successfully implemented in any developed society. The prosperity found in societies with developed economies suggests that free competitive markets are better suited than planned economies to improve the wealth of nations. It is an inescapable fact that competition in a free market produces inequality, and there is a very real risk that this competition expands the gap between the have's and the have-not's. However, this can be counteracted by a sensible tax system that does not undermine incentives to work, save, and invest. The fact that several countries are among the highest ranked on both the list of the most developed countries and the list of countries with the highest personal income tax is a testament to that.

Acknowledgement of the efficacy of the free market does not imply that we must subscribe to Nozick's vision of a minimal state. The so-called "socialist" Scandinavian countries have implemented progressive tax systems that make high earners pay higher income taxes than lower income groups. In some of these countries high earners pay more than fifty percent of their salary over a certain amount. Notably, the arrangement that, from Nozick's point of view, is tantamount to state robbery has made it possible to fund health care, education, and unemployment benefits for all plus many other subsidies without reducing people's incentive to work, save, and invest. Moreover, this redistribution model appears reasonably equitable in comparison with both the libertarian minimal taxation model and the socialist alternative of equal distribution. First, because it recognizes that in modern societies no one has a chance to become high earners in the first place without free access to a whole host of facilities already in place and financed by the community. Second, because the taxes make it possible to build schools and offer the public education that gives everyone a fair chance to succeed in life, independent of parental wealth. And third, because the system rewards initiative and success instead of handing out equal rewards indiscriminately to the work-shy and the hard-working alike. The crucial reason why countries that have implemented this model have proven successful, unlike those following the radical egalitarian Marxian dictum requiring from each according to his ability, to each according to his needs, is that they allow people to be rewarded and create wealth for themselves. The critical thing in terms of motivation is not that people are allowed to keep all their earnings to themselves but that they can excel, mark their difference, prove themselves more valuable than others. Parity pay is far from the same.

The Problem of Equal Pay

If we look at equal pay through the magnifying glass of sport, the insoluble problems related to it become evident. Originally, modern sports were played as pastimes by what the sociologist Thorstein Veblen has coined "the leisure class" (Veblen, 1994 (1899)). Participants were not paid. Quite the opposite, they had to cover the costs involved, which could be considerable depending on the equipment and facilities required. During the 19th and first half of the 20th century, amateurism was the norm, and many sports were only accessible to the more affluent. Not all sports were equally costly. Those who could not afford boats or horses could engage in less economically demanding sports. Thus, participation in amateur sports became as described by the sociologist Pierre Bourdieu a sign of distinction (Bourdieu, 1996). Strict rules of amateurism were invented to keep working-class people out of sports. For obvious reasons, unequal pay was not an issue in the age of amateurism. Instead, amateur sports were in themselves an exhibition of social inequalities.

However, those who tried to exclude working-class people from participation in amateur sports were unable to prevent entrepreneurs from arranging alternative competitions open for all. As a consequence, professional sports grew up alongside amateur sports. Cycling, for instance, became a professional sport soon after the invention of the bicycle. Bicycle manufacturers wanted to advertise their products and organized various cycling events to do so, such as sprint races, long-distance road racing and six-days races. Apart from the bike, what these races had in common was a sizeable pot of prize money, which in the nature of things resulted in unequal income.

For example, during the six-days race in New York 1897 the total prize money was $4,200 (equaling app. $128,000 in today's money). The legendary Charlie Miller from Chicago won the race having covered 2,092.5 miles. This earned him the $1,300 first prize (equivalent to $39,715 today). The one who finished last within the minimum distance of 1,350 miles received merely 75 for his effort (equivalent to $2,291 today), while participants who did not manage to cover this distance received nothing. Miller covered almost twice the minimum distance. So, the unequal rewards in six-days races could to some extent be justified by the fact that everyone rode for the same amount of time but covered different distances. But this justification was not applicable to other types of races.

During the Tour de France, for instance, everyone was supposed to cover the same distance. In this event, it is the one who spends the least time racing that wins and gets the lion's share of the prize money. Moreover, the winner is not necessarily the one who has suffered or exerted himself the most as the former cyclist, Paul Kimmage, reveals in his insider description of the Tour de France (Kimmage, 2001). Kimmage was a relatively mediocre rider who had worked hard to gain a professional contract. At the Tour de France he was what the French call a domestique. That is, a team rider who is not racing to win but to assist his team's captain in his pursuit of success. Still, in this unglamorous role Kimmage found the race grueling. At the end of each stage, he was completely wasted. Apparently, the race favorites were not. Kimmage mentions a disillusioning experience. After he had given his all in a time trial, he could hardly peddle back to his hotel. All his drained body allowed him to do was to grab the remote control, lie down on the bed and turn the television on, only to watch stage winner Bernard Hinault fresh as a daisy being interviewed about the race.

Hinault had beaten Kimmage by eight minutes on the 38 miles-long stage. Despite having spent less time racing, Hinault was handsomely rewarded whereas Kimmage, who had given his all for eight minutes longer, finished outside the money. Obviously this goes against the idea of equal pay for equal work. From this perspective, the distribution of money does not seem fair. Yet everyone seems to accept it. It may be tempting to explain this in relation to the term "prize money". The word "prize" signals that it is a reward won not earned. Prize money is different to earnings, because prize money is a bonus for an extraordinary effort or achievement. However, on closer inspection this explanation does not hold water. It is correct that prize money is bonus money, but the entire payment system in professional cycling follows the same pattern. Those who win races do not only win prize money (which, by the way, they often share with their teammates), they also get better contracts than those who work equally hard but do not win prestigious races. On top of that, race winners are usually offered lucrative advertisement deals, generous fees for taking part in show races etc.

The massive rewards dealt out to winners can be understood rather simply as a matter of market value. Whether we like it or not, the market mechanism contrives income differences because, simply speaking, winners are worth more than their less successful rivals. Although the market economy is meant to fit the ideal of equal-pay-for-equal-work, it does not because in most real-life occupations what constitutes equal work is, in practice, impossible to calculate. If we think of employees on an assembly line who work eight hours a day and carry out the same tasks at the same pace, it is plain to see that they all deserve the same salary. If owners of such factories decided to pay their employees differential salaries, it would be downright discriminatory if based on anything other than a transparent length-of-service scheme.

If we instead think of schoolteachers who teach the same number of hours and in quantitative terms have the same workload, it is still unlikely that their efforts and quality of teaching are the same. Some teachers prepare lessons thoroughly. Others do it casually. That is not equal work. Here, too, there is a distinction between input and output. Since conscientious teachers work more hours than their less painstaking colleagues, it could be contended that they deserve higher pay. On the other hand, preparing thoroughly does not necessarily result in better teaching. Teachers with a more casual approach may simply have more talent or a deeper understanding of the disciplines they teach. They can have an excellent understanding of the desired learning outcome and know how to achieve this without much detailed planning. Instead, when they turn up in class, they sense their pupils' mental condition and improvise accordingly. They do not spend much preparation time, but if the learning outcome of their pupils is on a par with that of pupils of colleagues who burn the midnight oil, it is hard to justify that they should be paid less. On the contrary, if they are better teachers, some would say they deserve more, despite working fewer hours. The problem is that, although most people who look back on their school days will recall good and bad teachers, teaching is such a complex activity that it is improbable that a set of parameters will ever be devised that could determine with any degree of accuracy who is the better teacher. One could be forgiven for believing that this explains why schoolteachers in a country earn more or less the same whereas professional cyclists, whose performances are plain for all to see, do not. But if we draw our comparison with football players instead, it becomes clear that uncertainty about what constitutes quality does not adequately explain why colleagues in a wide range of occupations receive fairly equal pay in a market economy.

Football is a team sport that requires a collective effort to win. Premier League teams consist of 25-man squads. Not every player in a squad plays the same number of games. Some are bit-part players, some play week in, week out. Yet, it is not the individual player's workload that determines the size of their paycheck. Player contracts are negotiated individually. When a club decides to swap a player, certain statistical features like goals per minute, number of assists, interceptions, saves, age etc. influence the valuation of the player. Statistics show what the player has done in the past but say little about future performance levels. Many high-profile players have flopped spectacularly after moving between clubs for large sums of money. Meticulous scouting and statistical analyzes of players do not erase the gambling element involved when a club signs a new player. And although there are a few star players whose quality and impact are beyond dispute, most often it will be impossible to find any clear correlation between players' salary and their contribution to the success or failure of their club. A brief look at the 2020-21 payroll of English Premier League Champions 2019-20, Liverpool FC, makes the point.

Top scorer Mohamed Salah who scored 19 goals during their winning season unsurprisingly tops the salary list with £200,000 per week. His attacking partner Sadio Mane, who scored 18 goals, is ninth on the list, earning £100,000. On the basis of impact, ability, and workload, it is hard to find any justification for the huge pay gap between the two. The player closest to Salah was midfielder Thiago Alcantara on a £192,308 per week. At the age of 28, Thiago signed for the club from Bayern Munich ahead of the 2020-21 season. Liverpool was strong enough to win the title without him, and for a long time he did not contribute much to the side. By the end of his first full season, he had made 24 appearances in the Premier League, scored one goal and produced zero assists. During the same season another midfielder, Curtis Jones, also made 24 appearances in the Premier League scored one goal and made one assist (Lfc History net, 2021). Despite playing the same number of games and doing better than Thiago in terms of goal and assists, Jones was on a 'meagre' £6,731 per week (Spotrac, 2021). Jones was a 19-year-old homegrown player, who had his first-team debut in 2019, which may well explain his comparably low pay. When the club wants to extend his contract, he will most certainly demand much improved terms for his signature. Be that as it may, for the 2020-21 season there was no justifiable correlation between the two players' earnings and their impact on the team. And the same appears to be true if we compare Thiago's salary with that of the established midfielder Georginio Wijnaldum. Wijnaldum is one year older than Thiago. He signed for Liverpool in 2016 and has been a mainstay of the side ever since, playing on average 35 out of 38 league games every season. In addition, he was instrumental in the club's Champions League victory, as he scored two goals in Liverpool's comeback in the semi-final's second leg against Barcelona. Furthermore, he was possibly the club's most influential midfielder in their title-winning 2019-20 season. Despite that, he pockets 'no more' than £75,000 a week. As a result, in the 2020-21 season, Wijnaldum (who, by the way, had featured in 21 of the clubs first 21 league games and contributed 2 goals) earned £3,9m while Thiago's total income for the same season was £10m.

If anything, these few comparisons demonstrate professional football's disregard for the equal-pay-for-equal-work ideal. And the same is true for the entire sports business. To the best of my knowledge, no established professional sport honors the idea of equal pay for equal work. Furthermore, there is no connection between pay and demands made by a sport.

In comparison with professional cycling races, which historically have been and still are organized as draining ordeals, football is a walk in the park. Nonetheless, an established World Tour domestique earns between € 100,000 and €400,000 (equivalent to $113,160 and $452,660 respectively) which is what talented teenage football players are offered by clubs in the English Premier League. In the 2018 season, the then highest paid professional cyclist ever, Peter Sagan, earned the record sum of €6,000,000 (equivalent to $678,980), which in 2020 was reduced to €5,000,000 (equivalent to $565,820) (Mitchell, 2020). And although such money ought to be more than enough to make ends meet, it is dwarfed by what the highest paid football players such as Neymar da Silva Santos Júnior, Cristiano Ronaldo and Lionel Messi earn. A leaked copy of the four-year contract Messi signed with Barcelona in 2017 revealed that the seven times Ballon d'Or winner earned up to $168,500,000 (equivalent to £123,092,197) per year (Kidd, 2021). Given such astronomical income differences between various sports and between athletes within the same sport, it is plain to see that there is no relation between workload and effort on the one side and earnings on the other. The income disparities are caused by marginal differences in physiology and technical skills, whose value increases to reflect the intensified competition between sport franchises. Clubs know the importance of recruiting the most gifted talents, as the margin between failure and success is thin. So, once they have identified a rare talent or want to add to their squad a player with proven quality in an area that they need to strengthen, they will often pay over the odds to secure the player's signature to fend of competition from rival clubs. The global reach and attraction of sport has further intensified the competition between clubs, since the most attractive sports franchises – that is the most successful ones – can increase their revenues at the expense of the less successful ones. While this situation widens the gap between the successful and the less successful sports and teams, it also increases the value of the most talented athletes in their respective sports and further widens the pay gap as well.

CHAPTER 4

Athletes, Gender, and the Free Market

Equal Pay and Athletes' Rights

There are those, and they even include club owners and managers, who think that athletes are ridiculously overpaid. In 2016, former Chelsea-manager Antonio Conte called the current situation "football's crazy age," and complained with some fervor: "Prices are too high in general; the market is crazy. When you try to buy a player, the cost is very expensive. It is not the real valuation of the player. It is a strange situation" (Smith, 2017). Be that as it may, as long as professional sport functions under market conditions clubs must either accept the order of things and authorize six-figure contracts or face inevitable demise. Apart from a tiny group of superrich sheiks who invest in sports franchises for publicity or for fun, club owners will try to invest their money wisely. They weigh up players' track records, development potential, nationality, age, and sell-on value before they table an offer. Nationality, which appears irrelevant from a sporting point of view, comes into the equation because of the player's potential following. A Chinese player, for instance, may be more 'valuable' than a comparably talented Icelandic player due to the two countries different population sizes, because the Chinese player's countrymen are calculated to purchase more merchandise. Therefore, it is not a given that players equally valuable in a sporting sense are offered equal pay. Club owners attempt to create a healthy business, so it goes without saying that they will sign players for as little as possible and sell players for as much as possible. However, the market is not static, and prices are not fixed, so, despite all the calculation, it is impossible to establish the right price for a player. Players who are sold between mid- and lower table clubs are usually cheaper than players who are sold to world famous elite clubs. The reason is, of course, that selling clubs know that elite clubs have bigger transfer budgets. The following description of the transfer situation illustrates this uncontrollable dynamic:

> The market can move values, of course, but so can the environment. Last year, Newcastle United was relegated from the Premier League, it knew it would have to cash in on its two most salable assets, the French midfielder Moussa Sissoko and the Dutch wing Georginio Wijnaldum. Privately, the club believed that 15 million pounds would be a healthy price for each player. When Real Madrid inquired about Sissoko and suggested, without prompting, that it would be prepared to pay twice that, Newcastle duly increased its valuation. When news media reports suggested that Wijnaldum might fetch 25 million pounds — and his two most active suitors, Everton and Liverpool, were not deterred — Newcastle did the same with him. Both players soon departed, each at the new prices. That is an extreme example, but at many clubs setting a price remains a matter of instinct, of feel. (Smith, 2017)

The situation referred to took place in 2016. In addition to the £25m Liverpool paid Newcastle, Wijnaldum signed a five-year contract worth a healthy £75,000 a week, which made him one of the highest earners at the club at the time of his arrival. In hindsight, despite having paid Newcastle handsomely for the player, he seems a bargain. Liverpool has signed several players for higher fees and salaries during the intervening time. This, of course, has been noticed by Wijnaldum and his agent. So, despite having enjoyed great success with and been a great success for the club, he did not, as had been expected, sign an extension when he approached the final year of his contract. Instead, he let it run down in order to become a free agent and increase his negotiating power. Rival clubs had noticed his constantly high-performance level and saw an opportunity to sign him without having to pay a transfer fee. Hence, he was not short of suitors who could afford to pay a higher salary than they would have been able to under normal circumstances. There is nothing that suggests that Wijnaldum was dissatisfied with the club or his role in the side. On 31 December 2020, the day before the transfer rules allowed him to sign a pre-contract with a foreign club, he made it public that he had no wish to leave the club. So, had the valuation of players been the same as five years previously, it would probably have been easy for Liverpool to negotiate a contract extension. But because the market in the meantime had been rising, he had gradually slid down to 15th place on the payroll behind a number of bit-part players. It is hard to imagine any football player decline a £75,000 a week offer, if other players' salaries were kept secret to him. With contract sizes in the open, the situation changes. When teammate after teammate arrives on a much higher salary than your own, you begin to feel undervalued. As one news report explained Wijnaldum's position: "He is not asking to be the highest paid player at the club, but he is one of their key players and he feels that should be recognized." The problem is not that Wijnaldum with his current salary cannot afford a mansion, run a Bugatti, fly 1st class on luxury holidays, and enjoy stays at hotels equipped with underwater view and swim-up. The problem is *thymos*, "the part of the soul that craves recognition and dignity" (Fukuyama, 2018, p. xiii). It was a tribute to his status at the club that he was among the first players on the manager's team sheet week in, week out, but the manager's reassurance of his importance and value to the team does little to satisfy the player's *thymos*. Being only the 15th highest paid player at the club hurts his pride. There is, Fukuyama explains, a tension inherent in this disposition, as it involves both *isothymia*, a "demand to be respected on an equal basis with other people" and *megalothymia*, "the desire to be recognized as superior" (ibid.). That Wijnaldum did not ask to be the highest paid player indicates that his financial demands were motivated by *isothymia*. Why should he accept a salary considerably lower than other first team regulars? As fair as this may seem, an element of *megalothymia* is also at play when it was reported that he wanted his contract to reflect his status at the club. His increased wage demands inevitably signaled that he felt he was worth more and should be recognized as (far) superior to the team's world-class wing backs, Trent Alexander-Arnold and Andrew Robertson, who at £40,000 and £50,000 a week were both paid less than him. If the club met Wijnaldum's demands, Alexander-Arnold, Robertson, and other players (further) distanced by the Dutchman and motivated by the same sense of *isothymia*, could be predicted to demand 'proper' financial recognition as well. After Wijnaldum moved on to pastures new (a £165,000 per week after tax package at Paris Saint Germain that Liverpool would have had to find £310,000 per week to match (Palmer, 2021)), Alexander-Arnold's wages were increased to £75,000, whereby he surpassed Robertson in the salary hierarchy. The dynamics of supply and demand in international football are uncontrollable and have, with the intensified competition, become a growing problem for clubs as it puts pressure on their transfer and contract policies.

A way to curb the upward trend in the payrolls of European football clubs would be to introduce salary caps, as in the American national football and hockey league (NFL and NHL) and, in addition to this, take inspiration from the Scandinavian labor market model, where wage differences for people in the same job are usually linked to seniority. This, it could be argued, would in different ways be beneficial for both clubs, players, and the sport itself. It would eliminate the rich clubs' ability to outbid their less cash-rich rivals. All clubs would have to find other ways to attract players, and this would in all likelihood improve the players' working conditions. At the same time, it would increase the excitement of watching league matches, as more clubs would be competitive. And while relatively equal pay levels would satisfy players' *isothymia*, there would still be room for *megalothymia*, as unique talents could still outshine their less skillful rivals and enjoy the superior status that comes with excellence. Besides the benefits mentioned, the proposal that player wages should be collectively negotiated and follow a fixed scale rather than be individually negotiated based on talent and quality would also fit the ideal of equality. The problem with this collective model is that it would necessitate a break with the free market, and this appears unrealistic in a globalized world. What makes salary caps feasible in American sports is that these sports do not face any real international competition. Should players be dissatisfied with the wage limitations introduced in the NFL – and note that players' wages are also differentiated within the cap – they cannot find a more lucrative league to play in overseas. NFL is virtually a monopoly. Still clubs have found ways to circumvent the cap which, I add in passing, has grown immensely since its introduction in 1994 in parallel with the expansion of the league's revenues. "Back-ending" contracts by applying most of the base salary in the last two years of the agreement to lessen the salary in the early years is one way to do this. (Perritano, 2021).

In football, salary caps will surely be even more difficult to implement and control, as there are attractive leagues in many countries, where clubs are in the market for the same players. If one nation's league decided to introduce maximum transfer fees to protect the economic sustainability of its clubs, the adverse effect would be that these clubs would no longer be able to recruit world class players. UEFA's introduction of Financial Fair Play (FFP) in 2011 was an attempt to implement a soft salary cap across Europe to prevent clubs from overspending. The then president of UEFA, Michel Platini, explained the initiative:

> Fifty per cent of clubs are losing money and this is an increasing trend. We needed to stop the downward spiral. They have spent more than they have earned in the past and haven't paid their debts. We don't want to kill or hurt the clubs; on the contrary, we want to help them in the market. (Goal, 2018)

Regardless how leagues' revenue grows, a club's economy will always be stretched due to the competitive nature of the business. "Even among elite European clubs, continued excessive spending within the transfer market has been justified by owners and executives as being necessary to keep the club competition competitive" (Goal, 2018). If this is true, it says much about how difficult it will be within a market economy to control the ever-increasing transfer fees and player salaries that make it so difficult for clubs to operate within the FFP regulations that they themselves have called for. Moreover, it makes it clear that players from all over the world are unlikely to embrace the idea that they might join forces to push for equal pay and thereby contribute to make their clubs financial sustainable. Competitive athletes are not easily persuaded that they should give up their right to negotiate their wages individually.

Equal Pay and the Free Market

Trade unions have been established in free market economies, but it should be borne in mind that these unions have been formed on the initiative of workers. Trade unions have been successful because individual groups of workers understood that their bargaining powers would increase if they joined forces. Because workers' skills were not unique, one could be replaced by another. So, if one person found an employer's wage offer unsatisfactory, a hungrier person would typically accept it. Organized union members on the other hand could not easily be played off against each other. Trade unions' strike weapon proved powerful enough to increase the income of both skilled and unskilled labor far beyond what ordinary workers could have hoped for, should they have negotiated their salary individually. This is why union leaders in the 19th century Europe were met with hostility from employers and outlawed by states who saw the labor movement as a threat to industrial capitalism (Hobsbawm, 1975). What employers were faced with was not an attempt to dismantle the liberal market but simply working men's adjustment to capitalist market conditions.

Highly sought-after wage-earners never needed union membership to secure satisfactory wages. This fact has become more and more evident with the growth of the economy. The compensation of chief executive officers (CEOs) in the 350 largest companies in America is illustrative. Without the help of trade unions, these American CEOs have managed to negotiate exorbitant salaries. In 2019, according to an Economic Policy Institute report, this select group of people earned on average $21.3 millions, or 320 times as much as a typical worker (Mishel & Kandra, 2020). Considering the number of students that graduate each year from business schools, one may wonder how it is possible for a select few graduates from the same schools to negotiate such excessive wage packages, but the reason is fairly simple. The board members who decide, think that the CEOs they appoint are worth it.

Salaries are not reflections of any fair valuation of employees' effort. In 1965, CEOs earned 'only' 21 times more than a typical worker on average. In 1989 this difference had increased to 61 times. It is hard to imagine that the work of the CEOs during the intervening 24 years had become worth almost three times more to the companies than the work of the companies' ordinary employees. At any rate, the difference between CEOs and ordinary wage-earners' salaries in 1989 appears almost modest in comparison to the gap registered in 2019. Nevertheless, nothing come of complaining that CEOs' wage packages have gone through the roof and pointing to the unfairness of the ever-widening pay gap between CEOs and ordinary workers. So long as boards of directors are convinced that they must appoint prominent CEOs in order to succeed or survive, cheaper candidates will be overlooked. New business graduates must prove themselves in lesser positions before they have a chance of being identified as high-quality candidates for those vacant top CEO positions that provide the opportunity to negotiate mind-blowing wages. In this sense, the recruitment of CEOs is similar to the recruitment of football players and other professional sports talents. The difference in ability between the best and the second best is often marginal but, as previously mentioned, so is the difference between success and failure, and this explains why boards both of sports clubs and of other private enterprises are willing to pay way over the odds to recruit their top targets. If a state decided by law to introduce salary caps in its business world, it would restrict its companies' ability to attract its top talents and would at the same time reduce companies' decision-making authority.

In the aftermath of the 2008 financial crisis, when vital investment companies were bailed out by states with taxpayers' money, governments around the world were called upon to instigate measures that could counteract the excesses of the market. But even in the wake of a serious crisis, when collapse of the financial market was a real danger, no government seized the opportunity to challenge the business world's right to self-determination and to outlaw questionable incentives that make business managers short-sighted and more willing to run risks. For all the shortcomings of a market economy, when it comes to wealth there is consensus in the western world that a model with open competition is superior to planned economy models in which competition is eliminated or strongly inhibited. This explains, in part, why governments are reluctant to put the market on a leash. Another factor is that the free market has become supranational, which makes it more complicated and dangerous for any national government to intervene unilaterally. With the dynamics of the free market in mind it is time to revisit the controversial topic of gender equality in sport, specifically the question of equal pay.

Equal Pay Between the Sexes in Sports

Gender wage parity has been on the political agenda in the western world since the 1960s. It has taken the form of laws such as the American Equal Pay Act, passed in 1963, which made it illegal for employers to pay employees of one sex lower wage rates than the opposite sex, and the Lilly Ledbetter Fair Pay Act, signed in 2009 by Barack Obama, which was to galvanize the law against pay discrimination undermined by a Supreme Court ruling that went against the woman the act was named after. But political initiatives against gender-based wage differences have not eliminated the gender pay gap. Despite the unlawfulness of gender-based wage discrimination, American women are still paid less than their male counterparts. In 2013, the difference was on average 23 percent (National Women's Law Center, 2013). What makes it so difficult to eliminate income differences is that equity is incompatible with a liberal market economy. The considerable income differences between the sexes clearly reveals that gender discrimination is taking place. Such discrimination can be prohibited by law. But the identified pay gap is not necessarily a result of intentional discrimination and so long as there is no proof of discrimination, anti-discrimination laws do not help. In capitalist societies, the setting of wage levels is a private matter, and politicians can decide minimum wages but cannot otherwise dictate employees' salaries, as employees are entitled to negotiate their salaries individually or collectively. This is why political initiatives to eliminate income differences in the western world have so far been in vain and why the issue continues to cause protests. The world of sports is no exception.

In March 2019, the U.S. women's soccer team took the U.S Soccer Federation (USSF) to court in a gender discrimination lawsuit. The women wanted more than $66 million in damages. The core of the matter was that the U.S. men's team had negotiated a different pay package and, according to the women, been offered a more lucrative deal. According to U.S. Soccer, the difference in pay structures was a direct consequence of the women's rejection of the same deal as the one the men had agreed to.

> Women's national team players are paid differently because

they specifically asked for and negotiated a completely different contract than the men's national team, despite being offered, and rejecting, a similar pay-to-play deal agreement during the past negotiations. […] Their preference was a contract that provides significant additional benefits that the men's national team does not have, including guaranteed annual salaries, medical and dental insurance, paid child care assistance, paid pregnancy and parental leave, severance benefits, salary continuation during periods of injury, access to a retirement plan, multiple bonuses and more. (Blum, 2020)

The women's representative maintained for their part that:

In the most recent CBA negotiations USSF repeatedly said that equal pay was not an option regardless of pay structure. […] USSF proposed a 'pay to play structure' with less pay across the board. In every instance for a friendly or competitive match, the women players were offered less pay than their male counterparts. This is the very definition of gender discrimination, and of course the players rejected it. (Blum, 2020)

The two parties' version of the controversy differs markedly. If the soccer federation's account is true, the women's team have prioritized insurance, security, and long-term economic safety. If the same elements are not covered in the men's agreement, it is understandable that the men's team have been able to negotiate a higher direct pay. On the other hand, if the federation has openly refused to offer the women the same deal as the men, it immediately looks like a case of gender discrimination. During the preparation of the trial, the women's team captain Megan Rapinoe revealed that a USSF lawyer had stated "during a bargaining session in June 2016 that 'market realities are such that the women do not deserve to be paid equally to the men's team'" (Blum, 2020). Although this formulation can be perceived as an expression of gender discrimination, the reference to the market reality indicates that USSF's unwillingness to pay the women the same as the men is based on an assessment of the two teams' market value. It is beyond doubt that the American female national soccer team perform much better internationally than the male team. The women's team has won the World Cup tree times since the tournament was established in 1991 and is reigning champion. In contrast, the men's team has never reached beyond the quarter finals. Its best result is an 8th place at the World Cup 2002, and the team did not even qualify for the World Cup in 2018. At the face of it, it seems illogical to pay a relatively mediocre male team more than a female team that produces much better results in the same sport, but the reason for this seemingly unfair distribution is straight-forward. The income that USSF generates from the men's team's participation in international tournaments is higher than that generated from the women's team. For example, in 2014 when the men reached the World Cup second round, USSF received $9 million from FIFA, whereas the federation received $2 and $4 million when the women won the tournament in 2015 and 2019.

During a deposition, the USSF President, Carlos Cordiero, was asked to clarify what he meant when he stated publicly that the US female players had not been treated equally:

> I felt, and I still feel to a degree, that the lack of opportunity for our female players was really what was at the root of some of their issues. […] The fact that the Women's World Cup generates a fraction of revenue and a fraction of what the men get paid is a reflection, frankly, of lack of opportunity. Women's soccer outside of the United States doesn't have the same de-

gree of respect. (Blum, 2020)

In his explanation Cordiero implicitly addressed the issue of thymos, the desire for recognition and dignity. The women are idolized football stars. They identify and understand themselves as football stars. Male football stars at top international level earn gigantic sums. In spite of the women's status within their sport, because they are born female, they are excluded from earning anywhere near such sums. The lack of the same opportunity breeds a feeling of gender dependent undervaluation that is further amplified by the fact that the players in the less successful male national team are being rewarded more handsomely by their joint federation. The explanation that the difference is due to the men's participation in the more lucrative male tournaments does not alleviate the women's frustration, as it simply emphasizes the fact that men enjoy an exclusive gender-based privilege. Perhaps the most frustrating thing for the female footballer is that the inequality issue cannot be resolved by demanding the right to take part in the men's tournament. For the American women's world champions would not be able to qualify for the men's tournament, even if tackles and other forceful physical contact were banned. The profound difference between men and women's football was carefully addressed by the former USSF President Sunil Gulati during his deposition:

> There is an absolute difference, which not everyone seemed to agree to, but do I think that it's less attractive or less entertaining? I'm not saying that. Or relative quality, I am not saying that. […] But I am also not saying, in terms of absolute level of – whether it is speed or strength, they're the same. I think most people would accept to that, too. (Blum, 2020)

The way Gulati formulates his opinion shows he is aware that it is controversial to express what is obvious to the naked eye, namely that women's football is not played at the same level as men's football. In preparation for the Women's World Cup in the Netherlands in 2019, Australia's women's national team – ranked 6th in the world – played a couple of friendlies. In one of these games, they played the U.S. team that went on to win the Cup. The Australian women lost 5-3. A couple of days later, they played the Colorado Rapids U15 boys' side in another friendly and lost by a bigger margin: 4-1. The result was an improvement on a friendly they played in 2016 against the Australian Newcastle Jets U15 boys' team. On that occasion, the Australian national team lost 7-0.

Colorado Rapids and Newcastle Jets are club teams. But national youth teams exist. If we accept that the American women's team is entitled to the same salary regardless of the difference in revenue generated by the men's and women's teams, it could be argued, based on the equal pay for equal work idea, that players in the national youth sides were also entitled to compensation on par with the senior national men's team.

CHAPTER 5

Women and Sport

Women Footballer's Fight for Equal Pay

In 1991 the international football federation, FIFA, introduced FIFA's World Player of the Year Award. This award was based on votes submitted by coaches and captains of international teams plus a group of accredited sports journalists. Only men were considered. FIFA's World Player of the Year Award was a global pendant to the prestigious European Ballon d'Or established by the French football magazine France Football in 1956, an award that also exclusively considered male footballers. The two awards merged in 2010 and took the name of FIFA Ballon d'Or, until the partnership ended in 2016 and the two organizations reverted to their original names. The winners' list for these two awards includes veritable brand names such as Sir Stanley Matthews, Eusébio, Bobby Charlton, George Best, Johan Cruyff, Franz Beckenbauer, Michel Platini, Ruud Gullit, Ronaldo, Zinedine Zidane, Ronaldinho, Christiano Ronaldo and Lionel Messi.

Many legendary players did not win either. The list of people who never got any of the two awards includes superstars like Ferenc Puskas, Kenny Dalglish, David Beckham, Michael Laudrup, Thierry Henry, Steven Gerrard, Eden Hazard, Arjen Robben, Frank Lampard, Kevin de Bruyne, Zlatan Ibrahimovic, Neymar, and the Uruguayan Luis Suárez, who is not to be confused with his Spanish namesake who won the Ballon d'Or in 1960. This list of names is a testimony to the extreme competition that contribute to the prestige of these awards.

In the 21st century, much has been done to increase and promote women's participation and visibility in sports. In 2001, FIFA began to name a Women's World Player of the Year. Somewhat belatedly, in 2018, the French Ballon d'Or committee followed suit with the launch of the Ballon d'Or Féminin. The introduction of female versions of the two prestigious football honors were attempts to improve the reputation and marketing of women's football. Whether it has served to increase women's self-respect, as we previously saw sports philosopher Jane English argue, is harder to say. When the Norwegian Ada Hegerberg, playing for Lyon, won the inaugural Ballon d'Or award in 2018, she was interviewed on stage by presenter, Frenchman DJ Martin Solveig. At the end of the brief exchange, Solveig asked Hegerberg if she could twerk. Only the DJ knows why he found it relevant to pose this question to a football player during an event that was meant to celebrate her abilities on a football pitch. Whatever his intention was, it seemed to confirm Cordiero's claim that outside of the United States women's football is not treated with the same respect. According to critics, Solveig's question came across as sexist, since twerking is a sexualized dance move. After the incident, Solveig went to Hegerberg to apologize for his faux pas, while for her part Hegerberg downplayed the situation, maintaining that she did not perceive the situation as intentionally offensive or a case of sexual harassment (Dawson, 2018). Nonetheless, it is inconceivable that any male winner would be treated in similar fashion during the award ceremony, and it is hard to believe that Solveig's inappropriate behavior contributed positively to increasing the prestige and seriousness of women's football.

The DJ's awkward question was not the only thing in the setting that could potentially do more harm than good to the self-respect of women. Football's award ceremonies are not gender segregated. Since the female honors have been awarded, female winners have been celebrated alongside the male ones. Whether we like it or not, this sets the female footballers' abilities in stark relief, as pointed out by the Danish sport historian Hans Bonde, who commented on the photo of the two 2012 FIFA Ballon d'Or winners, Abby Wambach and Lionel Messi, as follows: "Everybody knows Messi, whereas only a few know Wambach, and one could easily have placed 10,000 male footballers ahead of Wambach, even if the male physique was left out of the equation" (Bonde, 2013). Of course, this is a controversial claim from the history professor, but Bonde's assertion – that the number of highly skilled male footballers is vast in comparison to female ones – is undoubtedly correct. As the short and incomplete list above of male superstars who did not win the honor suggests, the competition is much higher among male players than among females. This inevitably influences the valuation of the awards. Here, women's football experts might object, claiming that they find many potential female contenders for the women's award. Nevertheless, if for no other reason, the fact that there are many more male footballers, top-level tournaments, and teams invalidates that objection. So, when Wambach poses beside Messi (or Hegerberg besides Luka Modric) with their respective trophies, they do not appear as equals. The female player is simply no match for the male player who is assessed to be the best footballer in the world. She can only stand in his shadow. If this influences women in general in any way, it is probably not in a positive sense. In all other walks of life, at least in the democratic west, it is taken for granted that women are as qualified as men. Against this backdrop, it appears counter-productive rather than beneficial to reserve special awards for women.

If the ambition behind the introduction of women's football awards was to increase the respect, prestige, and recognition of the women's game, it might have been more fruitful to introduce a women's only event, where women could be celebrated without being overshadowed by men. Or, alternatively, to fully integrate the female players by making the footballer of the year award gender-neutral. This second option would signal that, although (currently) men and women are not competing against one another on the pitch, the display of their skills, albeit in separate tournaments, are comparable. They can be assessed by the same criteria as male players, who are also not always compared directly, since they often play in different leagues, on different continents and in different positions.

The counter-argument, that women would never win the gender-neutral award, because men in all facets of the game are better than women, concedes that female footballers are inferior to male players. Those who have witness the sublime ball control, dribbling and shooting of Brazil's six-time FIFA World Player of the Year, Marta Vieira da Silva, whose ability and playing style has been compared to her countryman Ronaldinho, will have reason to think that this is not true. The alternative counter-argument, namely that women will never be able to win the award because women's way of playing football is under-appreciated in a male-dominated sporting context runs into a similar problem. Because this argument implies that women's football is notably different from the men's game and thus concedes that there is an essential – or at least a decisive – difference between the sexes in sport. This also runs counter to the understanding of the equal qualifications of the sexes. And again, Marta's way of playing football makes it hard to maintain that women's football is essentially different from men's football. Moreover, given the current *Zeitgeist*, there is reason to believe that sports journalists, players and officials whose votes nominate players of the year will apply a "relative quality" assessment in accordance with the viewpoint of former USSF President Gulati who – albeit in a rather convoluted way – maintained that women's football is just as attractive and entertaining as the men's game. That the sports world is ready to embrace the equality agenda and act accordingly was further indicated when the voting sports journalists in 2020 named Wolfsburg's Pernille Harder, who was runner up at the women's Ballon d'Or Feminin 2018, Niedersachsens Player of the Year, a title that previously has been won by players such as Kevin de Bruyne and Edin Dzeko.

It would undoubtedly improve the standing of women's football and help to reduce the pay gap between men and women, if men and women were assessed by the same yardstick and competed for the same honors. Since the main cause for the identified pay gap is that men's football has bigger appeal to football spectators than women's football does, the best solution would be if women were able to compete in gender-neutral tournaments. But since less than ten percent of registered football players in the world are women, and since the best women's teams struggle to compete against boys' teams, this option seems currently utopian.

In club football, French economists Luc Arrondel and Richard Duhautois have found that male professional footballers are paid on average 27 times more than professional footballers of the opposite sex. Yet, "this imbalance is not the result of discrimination but is rather due to the size of the 'pie' to be divided up" (Arrondel & Duhautois, 2020). According to the two economists, the budget of the French male premier league totaled €1.9 billion whereas the budget of the female equivalent was only a hundredth of that namely €19 million. The clubs' net profit is relatively small. Their main expenses are their payrolls. That is, "the players pocket most of the money generated by football" (Arrondel & Duhautois, 2020). In this light, a twenty-seven to one ratio in the men's favor appears relatively small. Arrondel and Duhautois do not explain why the ratio is not closer to a hundred to one. Player salaries are closely linked to the clubs' budgets, which depend mainly on television royalties, sponsorships, plus merchandise and ticket sales. In recent years there has been a huge upsurge in revenues from these sources thanks to intensified competition between broadcasting companies, and this, in turn, has boosted growth in the value of football sponsorships and an expansion of a global fanbase for the international top clubs. It is these market dynamics that have caused the wages of male football players to skyrocket. The same upward trend has begun to make itself felt in women's football. According to Arrondel and Duhautois, the overall budget of the best French women's league has doubled over the past ten years, following increased media interest in women's football. The aforementioned Pernille Harder's £250,000 transfer from Wolfsburg to Chelsea made her the most expensive female football player to date and is an indication that the upward trend in the valuation of female footballers is not uniquely French but reflects an international tendency.

It may be tempting to think that the football governing bodies and elite clubs' promotion of and investment in women's football is motivated by a growing recognition of the gender equality agenda. In other words, that it is morally driven. Their true motives are probably less idealistic. It should be borne in mind that professional football is first and last a business. As a rule, businesses attempt to grow. That explains the expansion of established tournaments and the invention of new ones, which has led to a fixture list so congested that it is hard to imagine more games being squeezed in. It also explains why clubs build new stadia or expand established ones in order to increase the number of seats. And why new initiatives to boost revenues such as the e-season tickets, which lure the clubs' global fanbase to subscribe to exclusive interviews and other material produced by the clubs' private television channels, have been implemented.

Whereas opportunities to grow the business of men's football are running out, the potential for growing the business of women's football is still vast. It is logical, then, that football franchises have begun to invest in this almost virgin territory in the hope that it will one day become profitable. For the moment, this is not the case. Despite growing revenues in women' football, in France "the league is increasingly running a loss which has increased by an annual average of 75% over the past five fiscal years". Although the earnings of women in French football are only a fraction of their male colleagues' "within the same clubs, it is often the men's team that keeps the female ones afloat. The same goes for the English league" (Arrondel & Duhautois, 2020). This being the case, equal pay demands are unrealistic, at least at club level, as they would force clubs to close their loss-making women's sections.

Female Attraction

The cultivation of men's professional football has been going on for more than a century, while professional women's football is still in its infancy. In England, where modern football was invented, Women's Super League (WSL) (the equivalent of the men's Premier League) only began as a semi-professional league in 2011 and was small, comprising just eight teams. Seven years later, in 2018, the WSL became a full-time professional league and is now made up of eleven teams. Some of these are established brand names like Chelsea F.C., Manchester City, Manchester United, Liverpool F. C., Arsenal W.F.C., Everton F.C., Tottenham

Hotspur, West Ham United, and Aston Villa W.F.C. Other brand names absent from the WSL, such as Leicester City and Crystal Palace Women, play in the second division in which only part-time professional status is required.

The established brand names help to draw attention to the women's teams and attract sponsors, but affiliation to world-famous men's teams and stars is not sufficient to swiftly create an economy of similar size. It will take time for women's football to catch up, but with the right strategy it can surely become more lucrative than it currently is.

In 1995, former FIFA President, Sepp Blatter, announced in FIFA's official outlet, FIFA News, that "the future is feminine" (J. Williams, 2003). This announcement signaled that the governor of world football understood that there was an unexploited potential in women's football and that the time was ripe to begin to grow this market. If popular culture is anything to judge from, Blatter's prediction appears correct. Since Sigourney Weaver, starred as Ellen Ripley in Ridley Scott's 1979 science-fiction classic *Alien* as arguably the first real female action hero, there has been a profusion of Hollywood productions with hard-hitting female superstars. It would be difficult to mention a single male hero whose fighting skills overshadows those of Beatrix Kiddo, played by Uma Thurman, in Quintin Tarantino's *Kill Bill* from 2003. In another famous assassin movie, Doug Liman's *Mr. and Mrs. Smith* (2005), Brad Pitt and Angelina Jolie star as a couple who marry without knowing that their partner, like themselves, works as a contract killer until they both get hired by their respective contractors to kill one another. The film culminates in a dramatic showdown, from which we learn that, if physically top-trained, men and women are equal when it comes to fighting. Biological differences are insignificant. There is apparently an insatiable appetite for movies in which women beat the hell out of men or cooperate with them as equal partners in every respect and in all capacities. In 2020, Netflix released *The Queen's Gambit* that became the company's most popular mini-series to date. It is a different genre, but it follows the same recipe, bringing a new facet to the heroine. This time the heroine succeeds, thanks to her strategic mind, proving herself superior to all the nerdy men who live and breathe chess.

The series is based on a 1983 novel by Walter Tevis. The main character Elisabeth Harmon, played by Anya Taylor-Joy, is an orphan who is taught the game of chess by a janitor in the orphanage. The story is situated in the 1950s and 60s. In the all-male world of chess, the extraordinarily talented girl becomes America's best chess player, and the series ends with her going to the Soviet Union as a young adult to win the World Championship by beating the reigning champion Vasily Borgov. The novel is inspired by real-life events. The Harmon character is in large part modelled on Bobby Fischer, who taught himself to play chess and, at the age of 14, became the youngest ever to win the American chess championship. Borgov on the other hand is modelled on the world champion Boris Spassky of the Soviet Union, whom Fischer dethroned in 1972. The massive media hype that surrounded the Spassky-Fischer match due to its cold war implications is also reproduced in the series. So is Spassky's sportsmanlike standing ovation after he resigned the final game.

Even though chess is traditionally a man's game, it is unlikely that the series would have attracted such a big audience had the main character been male. It is the introduction of a female lead character that brings in the dynamic. The game does not require any physical exertion. Chess players are rarely muscular or present a perfectly toned body. Grandmasters come in all shapes and sizes. The absence of physical demands makes Harmon's ability to dominate her male opponents more credible than it does when slim and relatively small female action heroes make mincemeat of sturdy male villains. An important feature that should not be ignored is that, despite the body having no significance whatsoever for mastering the game of chess, the main character is not just a uniquely talented woman in a man's world. As emphasized on the official movie poster, Harmon oozes eroticism. She is a gorgeous ginger-haired woman with big brown eyes and full lips accentuated by dark-brown eyeliner and blood-red lipstick. This is worth remarking for two reasons. First, because there is no indication in the series that Harmon's appearance brings her any advantage or favorable treatment. Contrary to Julia Roberts in Garry Marshalls 1990 movie *Pretty Woman*, for instance, Harmon's pass out of misery is not her looks. Both movies are Cindarella-like narratives, but the Ugly Duckling orphan of *The Queen's Gambit* manages the transition from castaway to celebrity due to her exceptional intellectual gift. Her erotic appeal fascinates and attracts, but it is her quality at the chessboard that wins her admiration and respect. The second reason is that it underlines the added value of erotic appeal, even in contexts where it has no function and could have been disregarded. The director Scott Frank could have portrayed Harmon as the stereotypical bespectacled chess player, with little vanity and less sense of dress and personal style but, had he done that, the series would surely not have been so enticing. The experienced movie director is perfectly conscious of what every marketing director, hospitality manager, sales director, fashion designer, stylist and plastic surgeon knows: beauty and sex appeal are valuable assets.

The term coined by sociologist Catherine Hakim for this dimension of human interaction is "erotic capital". She explains: "Erotic capital has a business value. Erotic capital helps sell products, services, ideas and policies in politics, the media, the workplace, sports, and arts" (Hakim, 2011, p. 4). When it comes to erotic capital, women have the upper hand. If women are naturally disadvantaged in competition with men because of men's higher testosterone levels, nature has compensated women by providing them with the power of much greater erotic capital, thanks to the very same hormone. As Hakim observes, there is an imbalance between men and women when it comes to sexual desire. Both sexes have a sexual need, but men's sexual appetite is, in general, greater than women's ditto. Hakim identifies this as the "male sex deficit". "The male sex deficit interacts with erotic capital to color all relationships between men and women, at home and at work" (ibid.). This is hardly a revelation. The male sex deficit is observable in many aspects of life, but the field of prostitution is, perhaps, where it is most blatant. Among the estimated 42 million sex workers worldwide 80 percent are women, and the vast majority of clients for the 20 percent of male sex workers are men (Lehmiller, 2018). The reason why Hakim can 'discover' erotic capital as a significant addition to Pierre Bourdieu's theory of economic, social, and cultural capital is, according to Hakim, that: "Patriarchy has worked hard to conceal this in a fog of moralizing that controls women's public dress and behavior" (Hakim, 2011, p. 5). There are few places where the denouncement of women's exploitation of their erotic capital is more obvious than when women directly profit from men's desire by selling sex rather and providing it for free. Hakim – herself a feminist – maintains that radical feminists have aided the patriarchy in its attempt to contain and control women' erotic capital "by adopting similar ideas to belittle women's allure," and by claiming "that it is a myth that men have stronger libidos than women have and that it is merely an excuse used to exonerate bad behavior" and further by insisting "that there is no real difference between men and women in sexuality, as in other areas [although] evidence goes against them" (ibid.). There are clearly women who actively take advantage of their erotic capital, whether it be by marrying rich old men, pursuing model careers or simply reaping the benefits of it in salary negotiations, where attractive people tend to earn more than less attractive ones, as economist Daniel S. Hamermesh has shown (Hamermesh, 2011). Yet, this is not something that women generally accept, and invitations to take advantage of it are commonly rejected and dismissed as sexist. In this light, it is unsurprising that the FIFA president Sepp Blatter was condemned by leading female footballers when, in 2004, asked how he envisioned women's football becoming more popular, he suggested that the players should wear more feminine outfits like they do in volleyball.

> They could, for example, have tighter shorts. Female players are pretty, if you excuse me for saying so, and they already have some different rules to men – such as playing with a lighter ball. That decision was taken to create a more female aesthetic, so why not do it in fashion. (Christenson & Kelso, 2004)

Blatter's remark plainly grated with the *Zeitgeist*. Not only that, but he had also misunderstood the rules. Women play with the same kind of football as men. However, if we disregard his ignorance and male chauvinist wording, Blatter's proposal is not entirely unreasonable, and he is not the first person to have proposed making women' sport more attractive by considering their dress code. His assertion that volleyball could have different uniform guidelines for men and women's volleyball was correct. In beach volleyball, bikini was formerly a requirement in competitions for women, whereas the men had to wear tank top and shorts. This was not changed until 2012, when the international volleyball federation, FIVB, decided to allow women compete in clothes that hid the hair and most of the body, in accordance with the demands of the religiously oppressive and gender discriminatory regimes that some of these women represented (Cherner & Hiestand, 2012).

Badminton is another sport where the idea expressed by Blatter has been aired. In 2011, the Badminton World Federation (BWF) announced a new on-court clothing rule that required women to wear either skirts or dresses. BWFs initiative provoked accusations that the organization was sexist. In view of the criticism that came Blatter's way for his proposal for tighter shorts, it should come as no surprise that BWF's proposal was met with similar criticisms. So why propose it? In the words of BWF's deputy president, Paisan Rangsikitpho, "It has never been the intention of the BWF to portray women as sexual objects, and nor is that what we are doing". He went on to explain that "women could continue to wear shorts, tights, or tracksuit bottoms beneath the mandatory skirt". In other words, BWF did not require players to expose themselves more than they did in the sports gear they were already wearing. All the women was asked to do, was to put on an extra piece of garment to enhance "the esthetic and stylish presentation" of the players in the hope that this would increase the popularity of women's badminton (The Associated Press, 2011). BWF expected that a more stylish outfit would attract more sponsor and broadcaster interest, which in turn would benefit the players economically, as it allowed bigger contracts and prize money. In short, it was an attempt to make the sport more lucrative.

It should be noted that the proposal for a new dress code came after the BWF in 2008 had introduced gender-equal pay in the Super Series. This move towards gender equality was well-received by most players. Few dared to question the fairness of this scheme. The Dane Peter Gade, one of the world's best badminton players at the time, would get a smaller slice of the cake if this proposal came into effect, and he was not happy. Gade was all for gender equality, he claimed, but in his opinion this initiative had nothing to do with that. "Those who make the big draw are primarily the men's singles and perhaps few of the men's doubles as well. But generally, it is the men's singles that make the badminton circus economically viable." He compared it with football. Here, too, it was the stars who were paid the most: "You would never say that the best female footballer should have the same salary as Ronaldinho. This is similar" (Ritzau, 2008). Now, a decade after the badminton player who topped the world rankings from 1998-2001 and again in 2006 confidently maintained that no one would ever suggest that female footballers should be paid the same as their male counterparts, people have indeed been going to court intent on forcing through gender equity in the football world.

It goes without saying that the Danish Minister for Equal Opportunities at the time, Karen Jespersen, disagreed with Gade. In her opinion, BWFs decision was right, and she called Gade's argument flawed because: "In football we talk about salary. Here we are talking about prize money. Salary is different. Salaries are determined by wage agreements. There can also be sponsorship agreements, and that is how it should be. Here we talk about prize money" (Ritzau, 2008). It should be noted that the minister makes the mistake discussed earlier by separating prize money from salary without considering that, for some athletes, prize money is a substantial part of their income. It is also remarkable how dated this 13-year-old reasoning from a female minister from one of the world's most gender equal countries sounds today. Jespersen represented the Social Democratic party. Despite that, we are left with the impression that negotiating wages in football, and elsewhere, on market conditions represents a form of status quo that should not be questioned, no matter what. Curiously, when it comes to prize money, she sees things differently. When an organization determines the level of its winners' prize money, she does not accept the law of the market and find it wrong if organizations decide to reward women less than men. The fact that it is the men's game that generates by far the greatest proportion of the revenue suddenly has no bearing. It does not concern her either that there are many more male than female badminton players at elite level, which means that the competition to get there is much tougher. In her opinion, the fact that it is the men's singles that generate the interest crucial to deciding the amount to be shared is immaterial. And she seems ignorant of the fact that, without the subsidies generated by the men's game, there would be no women's competition.

Unlike the minister, the organizers responsible for the introduction of pay parity may have thought that, in order to justify men and women receiving the same prize money, they ought to do something to increase the draw of women's badminton and therefore broached the idea of making the women's game appear more... appealing. At any rate, they soon learned from the criticism that rained down on the idea of the new dress code that what they had thought was a smart marketing idea was, in effect, a public relations disaster. Consequently, a few months after the proposal of the new code being shelved for further evaluation, it was buried for good.

It has not been possible to find a single public statement by any female player that was critical of the proposal for a new dress code saying that they would rather keep the status quo than be forced to play in skirts or dresses to attract more interest and thereby contribute more to the collective economy. It is apparently part of the gender equality agenda that men's significantly greater contribution should reap disproportionately less reward than the women's, whose sporting performance has neither the skill nor the appeal of men's sport and relies on its support to survive. At least so long as women's sports fail to attract corresponding levels of interest. The idea of exploiting women's sex appeal to increase the attractions of women's sport is deemed sexist and disrespectful. As Imogen Bankier, a top twenty player in the women's doubles and one of the critics of the new dress code, complained: "You can't make demands like that to make women more glamorous… it is ridiculous; tennis certainly doesn't have this problem so why should we have to put up with it?" (NBC News, 2012).

Assuming that Bankier meant that sex appeal was not viewed and used as a marketing asset in women's tennis, she was wrong. In 2009, three years prior to badminton's skirt and dress initiative, the organizers admitted that the looks of the players were considered when the prime-time Centre Court game schedule was decided. In spokesperson Johnny Perkins words, "Good looks are a factor". Asked for a comment, a source at the BBC, which broadcasts the tournament, did not take responsibility: "It's the Wimbledon play committee, not us who decides on the order of play". But he willingly admitted that "obviously it's advantageous to us if there are good-looking women players on Centre Court." And he added candidly: "Our preference would always be a Brit or a babe as this always delivers high viewing figures" (Andrews & Fernandez, 2009). Against the backdrop of the 2008 financial crisis, an ESPN commentary spelled out the logic:

> … at a time when corporate dollars and sponsorships aren't flowing as freely as they were, it's vital that sporting events and venues show a quantitative return on a company's investment. One tried and true way to do that is through television ratings, and one tried and true way to have good television ratings is by showing attractive people. (Granderson, 2009)

The truth of these words was confirmed in 2021 when Emma Raducanu who is both a Brit and good-looking played and, as a singles qualifier, surprisingly won the US Open. The final in which she beat Laylah Fernandez was watched by 9.2 million television viewers, exceeding the 7.9 million high for BBCs coverage of the Wimbledon two month earlier (Tandon, 2021).

One of the most prominent examples of the importance of female athletes' erotic capital in relation to women's sports is Russian tennis star Anna Kournikova. In her prime, she ranked among the twenty best tennis players in women's singles. She played approximately 130 singles tournaments as a senior player, reached four finals but did not win any of them, and none of her finals were reached in the prestigious Grand Slam tournaments. She did better in the doubles. She won the Australian Open Grand Slam tournament twice, with her partner Martina Hingis. Hingis was arguably the best female tennis players in the late 90s early 2000s. In 1997, at the age of sixteen, she won three Grand Slam tournaments, Australian Open, Wimbledon, and US Open and became the youngest player ever to top the world ranking list. Despite the different levels of sporting success enjoyed by the two players, they earned almost the same. At the height of their careers, they both earned around $15 million in total. Hingis earned $1 million in prize money, six times more than Kournikova, who in turn made more money from endorsement contracts. The *Sport Illustrated* journalist and author of *Venus Envy: A sensational Season Inside the Women's tennis Tour*, Jon Wertheim, criticizes this state of affairs saying that, "I think it's embarrassing when far and away your most visible player has never won a Grand Slam tournament" (Valenti, 2006). He does not explain why he finds this embarrassing, but, implied in his description of the priorities of the agent's "tennis diva", what he finds hard to accepts is the exploitation of the power of erotic capital: "I think they have done a good job of making sure that these women go beyond the sports pages, and part of that is sex" (Valenti, 2006). At any rate, Kournikova, or those responsible for branding her, showed other women in tennis how lucrative it can be to use one's erotic capital to increase one's marketing value. The effect is visible. Tennis has become the most lucrative sport for women to play. Nine of the world's ten highest earners in women's sports are tennis players. The American footballer, Alex Morgan, is the only one in the top ten outside tennis, and she just squeezed into tenth place, according to Forbes (Badenhausen, 2020).

The Protection of the Weaker Sex

At a time when gender equality is as high on the political agenda as it has ever been, the suggestion that women should make use of their erotic capital to increase the interest in women's sport in order to make it more profitable may be perceived as a deliberate male chauvinist provocation. Female athletes should not have to play on their femininity to get attention. In this day and age, spectators should watch women's sports for the same reason and with the same passion as they watch men's sports. This would establish the foundation for growing an economy that would enable female athletes to be paid sums compatible to their male counterparts. Then we would have true gender equality in sport. The fly in the ointment is the annoying fact that people cannot be forced to take interest in anything. Many people have not the least interest in any kind of sport and loathe their screens being filled for weeks with the Olympic Games and the Football World Cup, which in their eyes are futile sporting events. Those who watch sports are mostly men. Worldwide, 76 percent of sports viewers are men,

22 percent are women, the remaining two percent preferred not to reveal their sex (Lange, 2020). The audience that makes sport a moneymaking entertainment industry consists by and large of ordinary men who are passionate about football, Formula One, cycling, boxing, cricket, golf, darts or snooker. There are lots of options, so if spectators do not like what they are seeing, if they get bored, they switch to another channel or they switch the television off altogether. There is intense competition for these viewers' attention. The most attractive sports have been able to strike billion-dollar deals with private broadcasters, and their financial dominance is further strengthened because the visibility that comes with intensive media coverage also attracts the largest sponsorships. These are the tough conditions in which women's sports are supposed to grow. Spectators interested in sport cannot be forced to watch particular events. The only way to change their viewing habits is to persuade them that the alternative to what they currently prefer is worth their while. It is unlikely that men outside a liberal academic elite will be easily persuaded by gender equality arguments. The average person may sympathize with the gender equality agenda, but this does not mean that he or she will significantly change or expand watching habits accordingly. National public service broadcasters, outmatched in the bidding war for the most popular sports events, could begin to promote the equivalent women's events and thereby increase the visibility of women's sports. Contrary to expectations, however, research interventions indicate that increased exposure to women's sports does not result in increased interest in it (Scheadler & Wagstaff, 2018). Sad as it may seem, people's individual preferences cannot easily be manipulated to comply with political ideals. It would help the gender equality course if women increased their interest in sports and began to form fan groups that could passionately root for women's teams in football and other heav-

ily commercialized male-dominated sports. Women's interest in sports in general has, indeed, been growing since the 1970s, but women's interest in watching women's sports is not rising rapidly. Instead, women's growing interest in sports most often results in a greater consumption of men's sport. A study of female season ticket holders of men's collegiate basketball showed that these women's disinterestedness in women's basketball was a result of their male family members' influence over generations (Farrell, Fink, & Fields, 2011). Tradition undoubtedly plays an important part, but biological gender differences cannot be ruled out as a contributing factor. If we couple Hakim's observation of the male sex deficit with Charles Darwin's assertion that, "with almost all animals there is a struggle between the males for the possession of the female" (Darwin, 1981 (1871), p. 259), we may get closer to a natural explanation of why women who take an interest in sports often prefer to watch men over women's competition. Athletes at the highest level have been selected through an uncompromising process of elimination. When men compete at the elite level, generally good genes are on display (Deaner, Balish, & Lombardo, 2016). It is aesthetically pleasing, and there are convincing indications that this appeals to women. The most evident of these may be the glamor and beauty of male sportsmen's wives and girlfriends, for whom an acronym has even been devised, "WAG" (Wives and Girlfriends).

Male spectators' attraction to men's sports is different, but recent research has shown that this can also in part be explained by biological dispositions (Newson, Buhrmester, & Whitehouse, 2021). Male sports spectators identify with male athletes. Fans who root for a team often identify with the athletes that represent their club, as manifested by the purchase of club shirts bearing the fans' individual favorite player's name. They express a sense of belonging to the team, which in extreme cases lead to expansion of the rivalry that results in spectator violence off the field (Newson, 2019).

Men's motivation for watching women's sports is different. Since there is so much quality sports to watch these days, it is mostly family, friends, and local aficionados who watch sub-elite sports. There ought to be nothing controversial in the statement that the difference in the quality of women's team sports compared to the same sports played by men is not simply marginal. Advocates of women's sports have argued that, rather than being a disadvantage, the fact that women generally speaking are weaker than men is an asset in relation to spectatorship, because it makes the games slower, less powerful and therefore easier and more exciting to watch (Bodenner, 2015). If that was true, it would indeed be impossible to explain why women's sports are not the average sports spectator's first choice, alongside old boys and youth sports. The evident fallacy of this contention is revealed if we replace sports with the art of juggling and claim that it is more exciting to watch a juggler who juggles with three balls than one who juggles with twenty because the motions are slower and easier to follow. It should be clear from this that, although it is correct that women's tennis and volleyball have longer exchanges that can be entertaining to watch, the argument is generally invalid. The argument is an attempt to promote second-rate as first-rate. The lower level of testosterone in the female body means that women will always fall short in direct competition and in comparison with men in sports where physical strength and speed are major factors. Fortunately, the same hormone that gives men an advantage over women in sports gives women an advantage over men in another and more vital of life's games. It is an advantage that old boys and young male athletes don't have, responsible as it is for the male sex deficit. But it can attract men to watch women's sport in spite of its second-rate nature. It is this banal insight that former FIFA president Blatter and badminton's former deputy president Rangsikitpho consciously or intuitively referred to when they proposed that sportswomen under their various remits should dress more femininely. These men were apparently unaware of or indifferent to the ideological trend towards the dissolution of gender differences that led 20th century perceptions of women as the weaker sex to be denounced as backward. They had not noticed that the gender equality movement had been influenced by radical theories that did away with understandings of gender differences as biological realities. That biological understanding had been replaced by an understanding of gender as a set of socially constructed performative differences that needed to be nullified before there was any hope that true equality would be achieved. The suggestion that sportswomen should dress more femininely played directly into this understanding of gender performativity as a manifestation of a conservative mindset that wanted to reinforce the patriarchal hegemony.

CONCLUSION

The Problem of Squaring the Circle

With the odd exception, people want recognition, justice, equal rights, and opportunities. Ideally everybody would appreciate one another, share the available resources, and treat each other fairly and respectfully. Clearly, in the real world this is not the case. Everybody living in societies properly ruled by law enjoys legal recognition. But recognition in terms of respect and appreciation can only be taken for granted at family and peer group level. Across society, people compete for recognition. Here, recognition must be deserved if it is to count for anything. What complicates this matter is the fact that there are no objective criteria that allow us to determine what deserves recognition and what does not. You can recognize pianists, mathematicians, adventure racers, activists, burglars, smugglers, chess and ball players for their various skills and commitments, but you do not have to. Because there is an ethical dimension to recognition, few outside their own peer groups are likely to recognize burglars and contrabandists for their skills. But ethics does not come in the form of an answer book in which you can read what is and what is not fair, equal, commendable, and worthy of admiration. This should be clear if we return to our point of departure and consider the UCI's acceptance of transwomen's participation in women's cycling. The acceptance of transwomen signals that cycling's governing body value tolerance and inclusion. The downside of this policy is that it is implemented at the expense of the ideal of a level playing field, as research has shown that transgender athletes retain a 12 percent advantage even after two years of testosterone deprivation (Ingle 2020). In sports where physical strength is decisive, transwomen's advantage is even greater (Hilton & Lundberg, 2021). So, the adverse effect of UCI's compliance towards transgender women is that it erodes women's cycling as a protected category for biological women who due to their naturally inferior physique would be severely disadvantaged if cycling was organized as a unisex sport. In consequence, sports organizations must choose between inclusion of transwomen or the protection of women's sport as a category exclusively for biological women and thereby defending women's sport as a level playing field. It is plainly impossible to be inclusive of transwomen and fair to biological women at the same time. As we have seen, some people in favor of athletes' right to compete in the sports category aligned with their gender identity try to erase this Catch-22 by claiming that transwomen do not hold a biologically determined advantage over biological women. Notwithstanding the research that tells us otherwise, if gender differences are merely social constructions, as some advocates of transgender inclusion in sports argue, it is remarkable that, while we have seen quite a few transwomen succeed in women's sport, we have yet to see a single transman successfully compete at elite level in men's competition. Even though transmen are prescribed testosterone, which is illegal for biological male athletes to use, they are not able to catch up on their rivals who were born male. Accordingly, it should come as no surprise that the use of estrogen and medication that blocks the effect of testosterone does not neutralize the effect testosterone has had on born males who begin their transgender therapy after puberty.

At the opening of this book, we saw Dutch silver-medalist Carolien van Herrikhuyzen proclaim her willingness to surrender biological women's privilege to compete in races for athletes born

Conclusion: The Problem of Squaring the Circle

female only in order to accommodate transwomen like Veronica Ivy. Herrikhuyzen disagreed with the view of third-placed Jennifer Wagner-Assali, who vented her frustration over the erosion of the protected category. Financial rewards are limited in women's master cycling, so the financial implications of the inclusion of transwomen are negligible. However, if women succeed in their quest for equal pay in elite sports and if the associated sponsorship and funding stagnate or continue to grow, being a female football player, basketball player, hockey player, cyclist, boxer, or MMA-fighter will become immensely lucrative, and the temptation to pursue a career as a female athlete rather than a male one will be hard to resist. Admittedly, even if they could earn a fortune by doing so, few, if any, biological men are likely to want to undergo sex reassignment surgery if they did not feel assigned the wrong sex in the first place. Hence the threat to biological women's chances would be limited. But if sex reassignment surgery is not a prerequisite for transwomen to participate in women's sport, the lure of money could move some (second-rate) male athletes to consider accepting the required hormone therapy to get access to women's sport. If the diversity movement maintains its momentum, and tolerance and inclusion of all sorts of transgender minorities become even more accepted, there is the danger of this creeping tendency increasingly blocking legitimate avenues for talented biological women in sport.

Given these dilemmas, it is impossible to decide with any certitude whether from an ethical viewpoint it is best to accept the inclusion of trans-persons in sports in accordance with their gender identification or it is better to prioritize the physiologically weaker sex. The first would maybe contribute to the promotion of trans-acceptance in society at large, which in turn would have a positive effect on the psychological wellbeing of this minority. The latter would secure the protection of born female athletes from potential harm and unfair competition by keeping women's sport exclusively for biological women. As the current debate demonstrates, there are fiercely competing views on this issue. The growing cultural and economic importance of sport amplifies the significance of the outcome of this debate, which in the last analysis is a discussion about privilege and status. Because these phenomena inherently involve exclusion (a privilege would not be a privilege if everybody had it, and a status would count for noting if everyone was on par) they will always be opposed, defended, and fought for. And there will always be question marks as to the fairness with which they are accorded. So long as one person's privilege and status are seen as another person's lack of opportunity and disadvantage, they will never be peacefully negotiated. This may seem lamentable. However, it is the competitive nature of humans that makes the world go round and – for all the injustices it has caused throughout history – has made it a better place for our species than it was when we found shelter in caves and caverns.

REFERENCES

Acedera, S. (2017, 23 December 2017). The Top 10 Tallest Female Basketball Players in The WNBA. Retrieved from https://sport.one/the-top-10-tallest-female-basketball-players-in-the-wnba/

Andrews, E., & Fernandez, C. (2009, 29 June 2009). Babe, set and match: Why looks count for more than talent when Wimbledon decides which girls will play on Centre Court. Retrieved from https://www.dailymail.co.uk/news/article-1196155/Babe-set-match-How-looks-count-talent-Wimbledon-decides-girls-play-Centre-Court.html

Arpi, I., & Wyndhamn, A.-K. (2020). *Genusdoktrinen*. Stockholm: Fri tanke.

Arrondel, L., & Duhautois, R. (2020, 14 December, 2020). Why do women football players earn less? Retrieved from https://news.cnrs.fr/opinions/why-do-women-football-players-earn-less

Augustyn, A. (Invalid Date). Battle of the Sexes. *Encyclopedia Brittannica*. Retrieved from https://www.britannica.com/topic/Battle-of-the-Sexes-tennis

Badenhausen, K. (2020, 17 August 2020). Highest-Paid Female Athletes 2020: 50 Years After Creation Of Women's Tour, Tennis Dominates Earnings List. Retrieved from https://www.forbes.com/sites/kurtbadenhausen/2020/08/17/the-highest-paid-female-athletes-2020-center-court-takes-center-stage/?sh=2cc9a8e45eb6

Ball, C. A. (2014). *Same-sex Marriage and Children: A Tale of History, Soical Science, and Law*. Oxford: Oxford University Press.

Baudrillard, J. (1990). *Seduction*. Montréal: New World Perspective.

BBC News. (2021, 13 October 2021). What's taking the knee and why is it important? Retrieved from https://www.bbc.com/news/explainers-53098516

Beauvoir, S. d. (2010). *The Second Sex*. London: Vintage.

Bennett, C. (2014, 23 November 2014). A Gender Agenda: the effectiveness of quota systems in increasing women's meaningful participation in politics. Retrieved from http://www.internationalaffairs.org.au/news-item/a-gender-agenda-the-effectiveness-of-quota-systems-in-increasing-womens-meaningful-participation-in-politics/

Blum, R. (2020, 22 February 2020). U.S. women's soccer team seeks more than $66M in damages from U.S. Soccer. Retrieved from https://fortune.com/2020/02/22/us-womens-soccer-lawsuit-2/

Bodenner, C. (2015, 9 June 2015). Why Aren't Women's Sports as Big as Men's? Your Thoughts. Retrieved from https://www.theatlantic.com/entertainment/archive/2015/06/women-and-sports-world-cup-soccer/395231/

Bonde, H. (2013). *Fordi du fortjener det* (Because you deserve it). Copenhagen: Gyldendal.

Bourdieu, P. (1996). *Distinction – A social Critique of the Judgement of Taste* (R. Nice, Trans.). Cambridge, Massachusetts: Harvard University Press.

Brassil, G. R., & Longman, J. (2020, 19 August 2020). Who Should Compete in Women's Sports? There Are 'Two Almost Irreconcilable Positions'. Retrieved from https://www.nytimes.com/2020/08/18/sports/transgender-athletes-womens-sports-idaho.html

Brooks, D. (2012, 16 February). The Jeremy Lin Problem. *The New York Times*. Retrieved from https://www.nytimes.com/2012/02/17/opinion/brooks-the-jeremy-lin-problem.html

Cambers, S. (2018, 24 June 2018). Billie Jean King still bearing arms in tennis battle of the sexes. Retrieved from https://www.theguardian.com/sport/2018/jun/24/billie-jean-king-wimbledon-grand-slam-equal-pay

Cherner, R., & Hiestand, M. (2012, 27 March 2012). Beach volleyball dress code gets a makeover for Olympics. Retrieved from http://content.usatoday.com/communities/gameon/post/2012/03/olympic-beach-volleyball-dress-code-gets-a-makeover/1#.YIgvQOuxXUJ

Cherry, K. (2020, 30 November 2020). The Wechsler Adult Intelligence Scale. Retrieved from https://www.verywellmind.com/the-wechsler-adult-intelligence-scale-2795283

Christenson, M., & Kelso, P. (2004, 16 January 2004). Soccer chief's plan to boost women's game? Hotpants. Retrieved from https://www.theguardian.com/uk/2004/jan/16/football.gender

Collette, C. P. (2013). *In the Thick of the Fight: The Writing of Emily Wilding Davison, Militant Suffragette*. Michigan: The University of Michigan Press.

Coubertin, P. d. (2000). *Olympism, Selected Writings*. Lausanne: International Olympic Committee.

Darwin, C. (1981 (1871)). *The Descent of Man, and seleciton in Relation to Sex*. Princeton, New Jersey: Princeton University Press.

Dawson, A. (2018, 4 December 2018). Ada Hegerberg says the Ballon d'Or twerk controversy was not 'sexual harassment,' and she was just happy to win. Retrieved from https://www.businessinsider.com/ada-hegerberg-says-ballon-dor-twerk-question-wasnt-sexual-harassment-2018-12?r=US&IR=T

Deaner, R. O., Balish, S. M., & Lombardo, M. P. (2016). Sex differences in sports interest and motivation: An evolutionary perspective. *Evolutionary Behavioral Sciences*, 10(2), 73-97. doi:10.1037/ebs0000049

Deleney, T. (2016). Sportsmanship - A Sociological Perspective. In T. Delaney (Ed.), *Sportsmanship – Multidisciplinary Perspectives*. North Carolina: McFarland & Company, Inc., Publishers.

Dreier, F. (2018, 18 October 2018). Commentary: The complicated case of transgender cyclist Dr. Rachel McKinnon. Retrieved from https://www.velonews.com/2018/10/news/commentary-the-complicated-case-of-transgender-cyclist-dr-rachel-mckinnon_480285

Drucker, J. (2021, 13 May 2021). TBT: The Mother's Day Massacre—Bobby Riggs over Margaret Court. Retrieved from https://www.tennis.com/news/articles/tbt-the-mother-s-day-massacre-bobby-riggs-over-margaret-court

English, J. (2007). Sex Equality in Sports. In W. J. Morgan (Ed.), *Ethics in Sport* (2 ed., pp. 303-308). Campaign IL: Human Kinetics.

Farrell, A., Fink, J. S., & Fields, S. (2011). Women's Sport Spectatorship: An Exploration of Men's Influence. *Journal of Sport Management*, 25(3), 190-201.

Fukuyama, F. (1992). *The End of History and the Last Man*. New York: Penguin Books.

Fukuyama, F. (2018). *Identity: the demand for dignity and the politics of resentment*. New York: Farrar, Straus and Giroux.

Gander, K. (2019, 14 March). Huge Spike in Mental Illnesses Recorded in Millennials and Gen-Z, Social Media Blamed. Retrieved from https://www.newsweek.com/millennials-genz-mental-illness-spike-mid-2000s-1362669

Gnuse, R. K. (2015). Seven Gay Texts: Biblical Passages Used to Condemn Homosexuality. *Biblical Theology Bulletin*, 45(2), 68-87. doi:10.1177/0146107915577097

Goal. (2018). What is Financial Fair Play and how does it work? FFP rules explained. Retrieved from https://www.goal.com/en/news/what-is-financial-fair-play-and-how-does-it-work-ffp-rules/1ihlynh8s59i319l6nxx1z6kg5

Government Offices of Sweden. (2019, 19 November 2020). A Feminist Government. Retrieved from https://www.government.se/government-policy/a-feminist-government/

Granderson, L. (2009, 6 July 2009). Finding the beauty in ugly.

Retrieved from http://www.espn.com/espn/page2/story?sportCat=tennis&page=granderson/090701

Guttmann, A. (1991). *Women's sports: A history*. Columbia: Columbia University Press.

Hakim, C. (2011). *Erotic capital: The power of attraction in the boardroom and the bedroom*: Basic books.

Hamermesh, D. S. (2011). *Beauty Pays – Why Attractive People Are More Successful*. Princeton: Princeton University Press.

Hilton, E. N., & Lundberg, T. R. (2021). Transgender Women in the Female Category of Sport: Perspectives on Testosterone Suppression and Performance Advantage. *Sports Medicine*, 51(2), 199-214. doi:10.1007/s40279-020-01389-3

Hobsbawm, E. (1975). *The Age of Capital 1848-1875*. London: Wiedenfeld & Nicolson.

Horkheimer, M., & Adorno, T. W. (1969). *Dialektik der Aufklärung – Philosophische Fragmente Frankfurt am Main*: S. Fischer Verlag.

Howe, L. A. (2004). Gamesmanship. *Journal of the Philosophy of Sport*, 31(2), 212-225.

Ingle, S. (2019, 4 March 2019). Elite sport is gradually waking up to widespread mental health issues. Retrieved from https://www.theguardian.com/sport/blog/2019/mar/04/elite-sport-mental-health

Inter-Parliamentary Union. (2019, 1 February 2019). Women in national parliaments. Retrieved from http://archive.ipu.org/wmn-e/classif.htm

Jones, B. A., Arcelus, J., Bouman, W. P., & Haycraft, E. (2017). Sport and Transgender People: A Systematic Review of the Literature Relating to Sport Participation and Competitive Sport Policies. *Sports Medicine*, 47(4), 701-716. doi:10.1007/s40279-016-0621-y

Kidd, R. (2021, 31 January 2021). Report Reveals FC Barcelona Star Lionel Messi's Record-Breaking Contract. Retrieved from https://www.forbes.com/sites/robertkidd/2021/01/31/report-reveals-fc-barcelona-star-lionel-messis-record-breaking-contract/?sh=622f5ef75bcc

Kimmage, P. (2001). *Rough ride: behind the wheel with a pro cyclist*. London: Yellow Jersey.

Kohout, M. (2013, 21 May 2013). Women Lead the Way For Future Growth of Cycling in North America. Retrieved from https://momentummag.com/women-lead-the-way-for-future-growth-of-cycling-in-north-america/

Lange, D. (2020, 26 November 2020). Gender distribution of sports fans worldwide. Retrieved from https://www.statista.com/statistics/1114119/sports-fans-gender-distribution/

Lehmiller, J. (2018, 21 February 2018). Nearly One in Five Sex Workers Are Men. Retrieved from https://www.vice.com/en/article/evm5vw/nearly-one-in-five-sex-workers-are-men

Lfc History net. (2021). Lfc Archives. Retrieved from https://www.lfchistory.net/

Loland, S. (2018). Performance-Enhancing Drugs, Sport, and the Ideal of Natural Athletic Performance. *The American Journal of Bioethics*, 18(6), 8-15. doi:10.1080/15265161.2018.1459934

Marquis de Lafayette. (1789). Declaration of the Rights of Man and of the Citizen. Retrieved from https://www.elysee.fr/en/french-presidency/the-declaration-of-the-rights-of-man-and-of-the-citizen

Martschenko, D. (2017, 1 February 2018). The IQ test wars: why screening for intelligence is still so controversial. Retrieved from https://theconversation.com/the-iq-test-wars-why-screening-for-intelligence-is-still-so-controversial-81428

Matthews, G. R. (1980). The Controversial Olympic Games of 1908 As Viewed by the "New York Times" and the "Times" of London. *Journal of Sport History*, 7(2), 40-53. Retrieved from http://www.jstor.org/stable/43610353

Mills, C. W. (2000 (1959)). *The Sociological Imagination*. Oxford: Oxford University Press.

Mishel, L., & Kandra, J. (2020, 18 August, 2020). CEO compensation surged 14% in 2019 to $21.3 million. Retrieved from https://www.epi.org/publication/ceo-compensation-surged-14-in-2019-to-21-3-million-ceos-now-earn-320-times-as-much-as-a-typical-worker/

Mitchell, M. (2020, 20 May, 2020). How Much do Pro Cyclists Earn? Retrieved from https://www.procyclinguk.com/how-much-pro-cyclists-earn/

Møller, V. (2010). *The Ethics of Doping and Anti-Doping: Redeeming the Soul of Sport*. London: Routledge.

Murray, J. (2021, 6 June 2021). Tory MP to boycott England games in row over taking the knee. Retrieved from https://www.theguardian.com/politics/2021/jun/06/tory-mp-to-boycott-england-games-in-row-over-taking-the-knee

Murray, T. H. (2018). "Natural" Talents and Dedication—Meanings and Values in Sport. *S*, 18(6), 1-3. doi:10.1080/15265161.2018.1474014

National Women's Law Center. (2013, 29 January 2013). Resource: Lilly Ledbetter Fair Pay Act. Retrieved from https://nwlc.org/resources/lilly-ledbetter-fair-pay-act/

NBC News. (2012, 4 June 2012). Badminton shelves rule requiring women wear skirts. Retrieved from https://www.nbcnews.com/news/world/badminton-shelves-rule-requiring-women-wear-skirts-flna812049

New Idea. (2019, 15 November). Nike sweatshops: inside the scandal. Retrieved from https://www.newidea.com.au/nike-sweatshops-the-truth-about-the-nike-factory-scandal

Newson, M. (2019). Football, fan violence, and identity fusion. *International Review for the Sociology of Sport*, 54(4), 431-444. doi:10.1177/1012690217731293

Newson, M., Buhrmester, M., & Whitehouse, H. (2021). United in defeat: shared suffering and group bonding among football fans. *Managing Sport and Leisure*, 1-18. doi:10.1080/23750472.2020.1866650

Nike. (2017). Until we all win. Retrieved from https://www.nike.com/until-we-all-win

Nozick, R. (1974). *Anarchy, State, and Utopia*. Oxford: Blackwell Publishers Ltd.

Ostry, J. D., Alvarez, J., Espinoza, R., & Papageorgiou, C. (2018). Economic Gains from Gender Inclusion: New Mechanisms, New Evidence. Retrieved from Washington DC

Palmer, K. (2021, 9 June 2021). Gini Wijnaldum joins Paris Saint-Germain and says full story behind his Liverpool exit will be told. Retrieved from https://www.sundayworld.com/sport/soccer/gini-wijnaldum-joins-paris-saint-germain-and-says-full-story-behind-his-liverpool-exit-will-be-told-40522065.html

Perritano, J. (2021, 17 February 2021). How does the NFL salary cap work? Retrieved from https://entertainment.howstuffworks.com/question644.htm

Piketty, T. (2017). *Capital in the Twenty-First Century*. Cambridge, Massachusetts: The Belknap Press of Harvard University.

Pinker, S. (2012). *The Better Angels of Our Nature: Why violence has declined*. New York: Penguin Books.

Pluckrose, H., & Lindsay, J. (2021). *Cynical Theories: How Activist Scholarship Made Everything about Race Gender, and Identity – and Why This Harms Everybody*. London: Swift Press.

Politico. (2021, 8 March 2021). National Tracking Poll #210332. Retrieved from https://www.politico.com/f/?id=00000178-1a7a-d750-a77a-3efba0ac0000&nname=playbook-pm&nid=0000015a-dd3e-d536-a37b-dd7fd8af0000&nrid=0000014e-f102-dd93-ad7f-f9076e3c0000&nlid=964328

Rawls, J. (1971). *A Theory of Justice*. Cambridge, Massachusetts, London: Harvard University Press.

Ritzau. (2008, 10 January 2008). Peter Gade kritiserer ligeløn. Retrieved from https://www.dr.dk/sporten/badminton/peter-gade-kritiserer-ligeloen

Roberts, T. A., Smalley, J., & Ahrendt, D. (2021). Effect of gender affirming hormones on athletic performance in transwomen and transmen: implications for sporting organisations and legislators. *British journal of sports medicine*, 55(11), 577-583. doi:10.1136/bjsports-2020-102329

Scheadler, T., & Wagstaff, A. (2018). Exposure to Women's Sports: Changing Attitudes Toward Female Athletes. *The Sport Journal*, 21. Retrieved from https://thesportjournal.org/article/exposure-to-womens-sports-changing-attitudes-toward-female-athletes/

Smith, R. (2017, 22 June, 2017). Soccer's Confounding Calculation: What's a Player Worth? Retrieved from https://www.nytimes.com/2017/06/22/sports/soccer/premier-league-transfers.html

Spotrac. (2021, 1 January 2021). Liverpool F.C. 2020-21 Payroll. Retrieved from https://www.spotrac.com/epl/liverpool-fc/payroll/

Standing, G. (2014). *The Precariat. The New Dangerous Class*. London, New Delhi, New York, Sydney: Bloomsbury.

Stathead.com. (2011). Stathead Basketball. Retrieved from https://stathead.com/basketball/psl_finder.cgi?request=1&sum=1&type=totals&per_minute_base=36&lg_id=NBA&is_playoffs=N&year_min=1947&year_max=2011&franch_id=&season_start=1&season_end=-1&age_min=0&age_max=99&height_min=0&height_max=69&birth_country_is=Y&birth_country=&is_active=&is_hof=&pos=&qual=&c1stat=&c1comp=gt&c1val=&c2stat=&c2comp=gt&c2val=&c3stat=&c3comp=gt&c3val=&c4stat=&c4comp=gt&c4val=&c5stat=&c5comp=gt&c6mult=1.0&c6stat=&order_by=height

Stewart, J. (2018). Hegel's Theory of Recognition and Philosophical Anthropology and the Ethical Challenges of a Globalized World. *The Philosophical Forum*, 49(4), 467-481. doi:https://doi.org/10.1111/phil.12202

Stuff. (2018, 17 October 2018). Transgender cycling world champion causes a stir among her competitors. Retrieved from https://www.stuff.co.nz/sport/other-sports/107898970/transgender-cycling-world-champion-causes-a-stir-among-her-competitors#comments

Tandon, K. (2021, 14 September 2021). Emma Raducanu's US Open triumph garners blockbuster ratings on British TV. Retrieved from https://www.tennis.com/news/articles/emma-raducanu-us-open-triumph-garners-blockbuster-ratings-on-british-tv-audience

Tännsjö, T. (2007). Against Sexual Discrimination in Sports. In W. J. Morgan (Ed.), *Ethics in Sport* (pp. 347-358). Campaign IL: Human Kinetics.

The Associated Press. (2011, 4 May 2011). Badminton world body orders women to wear skirts. Retrieved from https://www.ctvnews.ca/badminton-world-body-orders-women-to-wear-skirts-1.639653

The Babylon Bee. (2019, 25 October 2019). Motorcyclist Who Identifies As Bicyclist Sets Cycling World Record. Retrieved from https://babylonbee.com/news/motorcycle-that-identifies-as-bicycle-sets-world-cycling-record

Thomas, L. (2021, 19 February 2021). Ivan Toney explains why Brentford players won't take a knee: 'We are being used as puppets'. Retrieved from https://www.skysports.com/football/

news/11748/12221923/ivan-toney-explains-why-brentford-players-wont-take-a-knee-we-are-being-used-as-puppets

United Nations. (1948). Universal Declaration of Human Rights. Retrieved from https://www.un.org/sites/un2.un.org/files/udhr.pdf

Valenti, C. (2006, 6 January 2006). Women's Tennis Draws Endorsement Dollars. Retrieved from https://abcnews.go.com/Business/story?id=87962&page=1

van der Toorn, J., Jost, J. T., Packer, D. J., Noorbaloochi, S., & Van Bavel, J. J. (2017). In Defense of Tradition: Religiosity, Conservatism, and Opposition to Same-Sex Marriage in North America. *Personality & social psychology bulletin*, 43(10), 1455-1468. doi:10.1177/0146167217718523

Veblen, T. (1994 (1899)). *The Theory of the Leisure Class*. London: Penguin Books.

Widlund, T. (1994). Ethelbert Talbot – His Life and Place in Olympic History. Retrieved from https://digital.la84.org/digital/collection/p17103coll10/id/3064/rec/1

Williams, J. (2003). The fastest growing sport? women's football in England. *Soccer & Society*, 4(2-3), 112-127. doi:10.1080/14660970512331390865

Williams, S. (2019, 11 August 2019). Are women better ultra-endurance athletes than men? Retrieved from https://www.bbc.com/news/world-49284389

www.ingramcontent.com/pod-product-compliance
Lightning Source LLC
Chambersburg PA
CBHW022131160426
43197CB00009B/1235